[handwritten] Amazing!t + God [illegible]
DJ,
ed_hird@telus.net

For Better, For Worse

Discovering the keys to a lasting relationship

by Rev. Dr. Ed and Janice Hird

HISPUBLISHING
GROUP

www.hispubg.com
A division of HISpecialists, llc

In this work, Ed and Janice Hird bring together their vast experience in working with couples, their faith, and their own personal growth and learning. They put all of this into the context of Bowen Family Systems Theory to make a readable and useful book for the reader. Highly recommended.

—Dr. Ronald W. Richardson,
author of *Family Ties that Bind* and *Couples in Conflict: A Family Systems Approach to Marriage Counseling*

Ed and Janice, as many spiritual/ nonspiritual practices share, made a vow/promise to themselves and each other when they were legally married forty years ago to honour each other. In order to keep their vow to themselves and each other, they did their personal work with a family and marriage counsellor.

Having utilized universal psychological/ spiritual truths to do their own couple work as related in their book *For Better For Worse*, Rev. Hird and his wife Janice have related in an authentic humorous story form their marital journey challenges of staying committed in their couple relationship of forty years. They worked their relationship out with all of its joys and sorrows while raising three boys, serving together in a church as well as Janice having her own career and Ed advancing his career with a Doctorate in strengthening marriages and writing books while practicing these universal principles. These truths can guide and serve to support you in doing your work to remain in a loving committed marital relationship as well as long as you are willing to do your work in your marital relationship "for better for worse."

—Bonnie Chatwin,
Counselling and Consultation, Dip. Nurse,
AAMFT, BCMFT, M.T.S.C, R.C.C.

I have known Ed and Janice for over forty years and have watched them grow, mature and blossom in their own marriage. This book is a great resource for couples who yearn for the *Better*. It focuses on the four key marriage principles: rediscovering strengths, celebrating differences, valuing conflict, and balancing closeness and personal space. There is excellent balance between the theory of these principles and the courageous sharing of real life examples by Ed and Janice from their own marital journey. Throughout the book one is challenged to ponder one's own marriage and then to forge ahead in the adventure of learning new marital dance steps. I will highly recommend *For Better, For Worse* to my patients, family and friends.

—John Cline M.D., B.Sc.

Christian marriage has never before been under such pressure from all sides. At the same time there is a desperate need in our culture for a radiant and working testimony to the love of God as seen in a fully-functioning marriage partnership. This book is both deeply thought-through as well as practically thought-provoking. It is based soundly on the proven, personal experience of the married authors as well as on their extensive research and their proven ministry in helping others to strengthen their marriages. We thoroughly commend it to you.

—Rev. John (and Anne) Coles
Chair – New Wine Trust Ltd

This book would be helpful to any married couple. Within its pages, Ed and Janice Hird demonstrate a sound understanding of Systems Theory applied to marriage, a breadth of knowledge of Biblical counsel on marriage and years of experience in teaching and counseling married couples. I highly recommend it to any couple who want a better marriage.

—Richard E. Campbell Ph.D.,
Retired Marriage Family Therapist

I have known Ed for almost fifty years. In his life he is constantly seeking to apply truth. In this practical book, he shares trustworthy advice for any marriage.
– David C. Bentall,
family enterprise advisor, professional speaker, and author of
Leaving a Legacy and Company You Keep, FFI Fellow, Next Step Advisors Inc.

1. This book records the honest, true and "trials and errors" accounts of how Ed & Janice discover the keys to their lasting marriage relationship. It is filled with records of life experiences and honest evaluations of the real questions that every married couple needs to face. It is worth reading, especially for married couples who long to develop a lasting and loving relationship.

2. This book raises and faces most origins and sources of marital conflicts realistically and honestly. It is a must read for anyone who feels called to marriage counselling.

3. This book will help to strengthen a new generation of healthy leaders, to provide wise and healthy leadership for the church today. It is a must read for all who are called to care for GOD'S CHURCH on earth.

My prayer is that this book will be used by God for the need of his Church today.

—The Most Rev. Yong Ping Chung
Fourth Bishop of Sabah
& Second Archbishop of
the Province SE Asia (retired).

A true authentic, non-judgmental story-telling masterpiece which will bring healing to many broken marital relationships, as well as to enrich many marriages. Ed and Janice's forty years of blessed marriage will help many couples to discover the keys to a lasting, fulfilling marriage.

—Rt. Rev. Dr. Silas Ng
Apostolic Vicar, Anglican Mission in Canada
Content Reader, DMin Program, Fuller Theological Seminary

The Hird's have been working on this piece with insight and passion and the reader benefits from their dedicated effort. Undergirding their thinking has been Bowen Theory which will enlighten your understanding of the family emotional unit and marriage. You will like it!

—Dr Peter L. Steinke
Author of *Congregational Leadership in Anxious Times:
Being Calm and Courageous No Matter What*

Marriage is the greatest institution established by God and the backbone of every society and nation, yet it has been under attack ever since it was created. Contending for marriage and family destiny should be our priority. Stable marriages and families are the foundations of peace. Rev. Ed Hird's book on marriage emphasizes that revolutionary love in marriage is the greatest anchor on which peace and oneness in the family stands. *For Better, For Worse* is very helpful to married couples to mend their marriages, keep the marriage romantic covenant love alive, and very helpful to those getting married as it gives them tips on how to revolutionize their marriage. You will not put this book down when you hold it and I promise you that you will never, never, never be the same again. I highly endorse this terrific book.

Rev. Canon Dr. Medad Birungi
Founder & President, World Shine Ministries, Uganda

For Better, For Worse is an excellent book that every couple should read. The principles shared address the issues that every married couple can relate to. Ed and Janice combine biblical principles and their personal journey in a masterful way which informs and inspires the reader to pursue a better marriage. This book will help married couples strengthen their relationship and bring greater understanding to many of the issues every couple faces. It is a must read for every married couple and anyone who desires to enter into a marriage relationship. The principles in this book can be used and implemented in counselling sessions as well as in marriage seminars. Well done Ed and Janice!

—Rev. Giulio and Lina Gabeli,
Westwood Church, Coquitlam

Your book is wonderful and will help lots of people. I applaud your work, your insights and your enduring marriage. The ideas in this book will help so many people. Your writing style is wonderful and authentic. I am encouraged with your powerful concepts and stories.

—Dr. Gil Stieglitz
Discipleship Groups Pastor, Bayside Church
Author of *Marital Intelligence,* www.ptlb.com

For Better For Worse is another "health" book from the Hird pen, building on two previous books looking at the health of the nation and church in *Battle for the Soul of Canada,* and personal health in *Restoring Health: Body, Soul, and Spirit.* This time Ed's wife Janice is co-author as they tackle a strategic topic that impacts all of us, and is dear to God's heart; health in marriage. In our world where there is increasing division, conflict and hostility at so many levels, Ed and Janice offer us a resource in dealing with relationships in general, and marriage in particular. They draw on practical principles revealed in the Scriptures and from their wealth of experience and expertise developed over years through studies, workshops, pastoral ministry and growing together in their own marriage. They share from their ups and downs with humility and honesty speaking to couples who are interested in strengthening their marriage, and to those needing help and intervention.

—Rev. Dr. Rod Ellis,
author of *King of Hearts*

For Better, For Worse: discovering the keys to a lasting relationship

Published by His Publishing Group

Library of Congress Control Number: 2018936419

Print ISBN: 978-0-9782022-3-1

e-book ISBN: 978-0-9782022-4-8

Unless otherwise specifi d, allscriptur e quotations are from the Holy Bible, New International Version*. NIV* Copyright @ 1973, 1978, 1984 by International Bible Society. Used by permission of Zondervan.

HISPUBLISHING
GROUP

4310 Wiley Post Rd. Suite 201
Addison, TX 75001
Ph 888.311.0811 Fax 214.856.8256

His Publishing Group is a division of Human Improvement Specialists, LLC.
For information, visit www.hispubg.com or contact publisher at info@hispubg.com

Book design by Wm. Glasgow Design, Abbotsford, BC.
Printed in Canada

Table of Contents

Foreword

I knew a married couple who had been together for twelve years. Their marriage was never perfect, and their arguments never stopped—mainly because they never had enough money to pay their bills. In the end, the wife decided to end the marriage simply because, she claimed, God "told her" to divorce. A few months later, God "told her" to move in with another man.

The Church today is full of stories like this. While there are certainly a few justifiable reasons for ending a marriage, way too many Christians are taking the easy road to divorce and paving the way for others with their bad examples.

That's why I am so thankful for the Hirds' new book, *For Better, For Worse*. Ed and Janice write from forty years of faithful devotion, and their counsel is both solidly biblical and pastorally compassionate. This is a book we desperately need today, at a time when the very basic concept of marriage is being redefined and people are trying to rewrite every rule.

Many today have discarded the idea that holy matrimony is meant to be for a lifetime. In my thirty-three years of marriage I've heard every possible excuse to rush to a divorce lawyer. Some of those excuses include the following:

> *"We never should have married in the first place."* Couples who are in love can make foolish decisions, for sure. Some hurriedly elope without any pre-marital counselling, while others aren't financially ready—so marriage becomes a nightmare of stress and unpaid bills. But once you choose to marry, you must assume the responsibility of adulthood. You must grow up and accept the consequences of your choices. If you shirk your responsibility now by bailing out, you will end up running from maturity the rest of your life.
>
> *"We've grown apart."* This is a classic line, but the accurate translation is, "I'm copping out." It's also an indication

that marriage is based more on fluffy romantic feelings than a solid covenant commitment. Satan loves to divide—and he will use suspicion, mistrust, anger, bitterness, and abusive words to create a toxic environment in your home. We must never give the devil this opportunity by listening to his lies. Jesus can reconnect a couple who have drifted apart.

"We argue too much." Married couples in the Bible had disagreements—including Abraham and Sarah, the father and mother of our faith. Arguing is actually healthier than burying your emotions—as long as you know how to resolve a conflict and let go of anger quickly. If you and your spouse argue constantly, it could be a sign that you don't manage stress well or that one or both of you need some new communication skills. Finding a new spouse will not fix your problem if the problem is you!

"Counselling didn't help." Estranged couples should always pursue counselling before calling it quits. But if your marriage has been in trouble for years, three one-hour sessions with a pastor will not fix your problems overnight. Counsellors are not magicians. If your marriage is in shambles, it will take some time to repair it. It may take months just to clear away the debris before you can rebuild. (And reading this book will definitely help in the process!)

"God told me to marry someone else." This is the most laughably absurd excuse I've ever heard. It's sad that God is blamed for such foolishness. If you ever think God is telling you to do something that clearly contradicts the Bible, you are under the influence of a deceiving spirit. Please humble yourself and get help immediately.

Whether you are currently single, happily married, or struggling in your marriage, this book *For Better, For Worse* will help you build a strong foundation so that your marriage will survive the storms of life. As you read this excellent book, invite the Holy Spirit to expose any weak areas that need to be repaired.

Open your heart as you open to the first chapter. Don't let any foolish lies or excuses destroy your connection to your spouse. And when you finish the book, reinforce your decision to view your marriage not as a flippant choice but as a rock-solid covenant that can never be broken.

J. Lee Grady
Author, *Set My Heart on Fire*
Director, The Mordecai Project
Former editor, *Charisma* magazine

Preface

Kneeling at the communion rail with her ex-husband, Linda said to her priest, Ed, "Someday I would like to marry Lloyd again." As Linda had said this several times before in previous sessions—and Lloyd had said the same—Ed said "Why not now?" She replied, "Sure, why not?" Everyone was thrilled that the communion unexpectedly concluded with a romantic marriage service. Linda and Lloyd had been divorced for six years before remarrying that day.[1] We will never forget that wedding celebration. Linda and Lloyd later took part in our Strengthening Marriage Workshop, and discovered new ways to improve their relationship.

What if we told you that this book, if you put its principles into practice, would send you on a romantic adventure with your beloved? What if we told you that, by reading and applying this book, you would discover the keys to a lasting satisfying relationship? Marriage is very important to Ed and Janice (authors of this book and organizers of the Strengthening Marriage Workshop). We have learned much in forty years of marriage, for better and for worse at times, and want to help other couples benefit from our discoveries about how to have a lasting, fulfilling marriage. Marriages back in 1911, because of health issues, only lasted an average of twenty-eight years.[2] Because people are living longer nowadays, marriages take more time to reach the finish line of 'till death do us part.' Today's life-long marriage has gone from a half-marathon to a full marathon or even longer. Your longer life gives you many more occasions to make mistakes and irritate your wonderful spouse, till death do you part.

We have made many painful mistakes so far in our forty-year marriage marathon. In *For Better, for Worse*, we pull back the veil on our imperfect marriage and share some of our embarrassing and often humorous moments. Authentic, non-judgmental story-telling is one of the keys to healing of relationships, especially in marriage. Too many marriages nowadays crash and burn. It doesn't have to be that way. Are you willing to try an experiment on how to do relationships in a whole new way? Would you like to end the cycle of broken relationships and marriages among your family and friends? Healing can start with you. You may remember how the Great Physician asked the probing question "Do you want to be well?"[3] Do you want your present or future marriage to be whole and healthy? Sometimes couples don't want to make the effort to become healthy. It seems too much trouble.

This book is written for married couples, engaged couples, and those interested in being married one day. Ed and Janice learned extensively about Family Systems Theory while Ed was doing his doctorate. This book integrates family and biblical wisdom about how to strengthen one's marriage and relationships. Each of the seventeen chapters unpacks key elements of what a healthy marriage can look like. The first four chapters cover the four weeks of the Strengthening Marriage Workshop, developed during the doctoral studies. The fourfold focus of these four weeks is on strengths, differences, conflict, and intimacy. Even if you read and apply just the first four chapters, you will gain new eyes to understand your marriage relationship in a brand-new way. Are you tired of seeing your partner with the same old eyes? Would you like to discover who they really are, beyond the mask?

To say "for better, for worse" sounds very romantic on the wedding day. To live it out 'til death do us part is much more challenging. Many couples naively think that because of their loving feelings toward each other, they won't face the "for worse" part. Do we have the courage to radically embrace the gift and challenge of the marriage vows "for better, for worse"? Marital joy is a deep joy that spills over into every corner of a family. Marital pain, likewise, is a deep family pain. We know of few families who have not experienced both joy and deep pain in their primary relationships. Has this been the case for your family? This book is about coming alongside people who long for more stable and satisfying marriages. Throughout the book, questions are asked that you can work on, perhaps through journaling and, at the right time, through sharing with your partner. Thoughtful questions can take your relationship to a whole new level of intimacy. If you even half-embrace the principles in this book, your marriage will never be the same.

Ed fondly remembers the first year of his forty-year marriage. Janice was the love of his life and the joy of his heart. As mentioned in the romantic Song of Songs, she had stolen his heart with one glance of her eyes.[4] Ed hit the jackpot when he married her. He was living his dream, working on his master's degree with his wonderful wife by his side. Life couldn't be better. Janice, however, found the first year of marriage painful. Everything had to be Ed's way. So it was his way, but Janice wasn't very happy about it. Being kind, she didn't tell him this until years later. Janice was working, and Ed was going to school. We were trying to save money to go to Europe and Israel before we had children. So, even though we were supposed to be sharing the money, Janice felt resentful that Ed didn't want her buying clothes or going out to restaurants. Because he was studying, we couldn't have a TV, and Janice had to be quiet in our one-room apartment. Ed was pretty rigid and dominant. Without realizing it, he was taking self from his wife, diminishing her unique personality.

Ed's first degree was in social work. There is a joke that after the first year of social work studies, you will try out the counselling techniques that you have learned on your spouse, and after the summer break you will come back divorced and wanting to be a marriage counsellor. Ed thought it was a ridiculous joke—until people came back the second year of social work and wanted to do that. Ed naively decided to try out his new counselling techniques on Janice. Fortunately, Janice was very forgiving. She said, "Stop asking me questions." When Ed started listening to her, it brought a shift in their new marriage. That was a lesson that when you are learning new skills, you often learn them awkwardly. It takes time to integrate new insights. That is why we want to encourage you to be gracious to each other when you are learning about Family Systems Theory because these may be new skills. Sometimes you can drive people to distraction with new things that you are learning. In applying this book to your marriage, you will want to be gentle and humble. Please don't use these new insights as a club to get your own way.

Over six years ago, Ed went for twenty sessions with a clinical Christian counsellor, Bonnie Chatwin, to grow in this area of gentleness. It is too easy to be blind to our own pushiness, particularly when stressed. Ed naively thought that he could get it all done in just two or three sessions.[5] Janice has also been to Bonnie Chatwin, sometimes with Ed and sometimes by herself. Both Ed and Janice have learned through the counselling process to be less opinionated and more willing to accept each other's influence. Have you ever been to a counsellor or marital coach? What was that like for you? Would you and/or your spouse be willing to consider going to a counsellor/coach? It is remarkable how much people spend on obtaining a divorce that they could have spent on counselling appointments. Divorce is far more expensive than counselling. Would you be willing to go for even one session? What do you have to lose?

Janice used to hold on to every offence: He did this, and he did that. It did not impress her when Ed initially left dirty socks on the floor, and didn't squeeze the toothpaste tube the right way. After a while, she realized she needed to "just let it go, because you can get all upset inside, but it doesn't make you happy, and it doesn't make him happy. Why not just let it go and don't sweat the small stuff." So, she learned to do that.

Every day we can irritate each other. So, we just have to forgive each other all the time, and it works fine. As Janice grew up, her family was never really taught to say "Sorry." Instead they would just say "It's okay." In Ed's family, they would just make excuses or say "No big deal."

Over the years we went to several conferences where the speakers would bring up forgiveness and how it could make you feel better to forgive people as Jesus forgives us. We were challenged by Jesus' teaching to forgive people not just seven times but seventy times seven. Jesus also said that if you forgive others from the heart, He can forgive you and it will break the chains off you. At the heart of the marriage covenant is the gift of forgiveness. Have you noticed that *give* is at the heart of the word *for-give*? To forgive is to completely give our resentments to the Lord.[6] Are you longing for a change of heart in your marriage? What might it look like for you to completely open your heart in forgiveness to your spouse?

God, as a covenant maker, is passionate about strengthening the marriage covenant. We are convinced that marriages are worth investing in, for better, for worse. In the past number of years, we have received a fresh conviction that what was meant for evil, God has meant for good.[7] Our marital pain has not been wasted. Would you be open to discovering the keys to a lasting relationship?

Many couples are trapped in secrecy and shame, unwilling to admit that they have challenges in their marriage. In some cultures, it is shameful to go for counselling. This might bring a loss of face and dishonour one's wider family. Appearances are often more important than being healthy. It seems like someone has to go first in working on their marriage in order to give courage to other struggling couples who are holding back from getting help. Through three decades of serving on Vancouver's North Shore, we have seen numerous couples who are high functioning at work but are far less functional in their marriages. Ray Anderson and Dennis Guernsey, authors of *On Being Family*, observe that marriage and human sexuality together constitute the greatest crisis for modern society. The very skills that make a successful entrepreneur often backfire in the living room and the bedroom, with such people being "totally lost when dealing with intimate relationships."[8] Dr. Murray Bowen, founder of *Family Systems Theory*, commented,

> In another group, a section of the intellect functions well on impersonal subjects; they can be brilliant academically, while their emotionally-directed personal lives are chaotic.[9]

The stand for biblical marriage taken by our North Shore congregation, in the midst of the historic Anglican realignment, gave us a visible platform and presence regarding strengthening marriages.[10] St. Simon's North Vancouver has developed a reputation of being a place where many marriages have been healed over the years. It has been prophetically called a wellspring of healing.[11] St. Simon's is a congregation that believes in marriage. The Bible says that in the last days, people will be forbidden to marry.[12] While people are not yet being forbidden to marry, it seems there are more obstacles than ever before. Some of these impediments are self-imposed. We have heard couples tell us about their expectations that tens of thousands of dollars have to be spent on the wedding and reception, that they must already own property, that they must have their education completed and their careers secured, and that they have to be able to afford a honeymoon in Hawaii. We told one of these couples that it didn't have to be so complicated. If they wished to get married, we could take their wedding in the living room of their grandparents' apartment. They took us up on the offer and had a wonderful wedding before flying off to Mexico for the honeymoon. Some younger people are afraid to get married in case they end up divorced like their parents. Marriage seems to many as either unattainable or unnecessary. We know of people with a partner and children who tell us that they are not ready for such a big commitment as marriage. Studies indicate, however, that marriage can bring greater overall health than other relationships:

> The Center for Disease Control and Prevention and the National Center for Health Statistics (NCHS) reviewed health data gathered from more than 127,000 adults from 1999 to 2002. Regardless of age, sex, race, education, income, or nationality, married adults were least likely to be in poor health, suffer serious psychological distress and smoke or drink heavily.[13]

Strengthened marriages can give hope to the new generation of healthy leaders. The Achilles heel of many gifted leaders is their sometimes-neglected marriage relationship. We are believing that this book will have a radical impact on next-generation marriages. John and Anne Coles, UK New Wine leaders, commented,

> It would seem that many in today's generation have seen little that would attract them to marriage. But we believe that as a couple work at their marriage, it can become such a source of beauty, power and strength that we not only find hope for ourselves but also offer it to the next generation.[14]

What if we told you that understanding emotional cutoff is at the heart of a healthy marriage? Dr. Murray Bowen called emotional cutoff the "process of separation, isolation, withdrawal, running away, or denying the importance of the parental family." He is widely recognized, even by his critics, as one of the key founders of the field of marriage and family therapy.[15] In 1975, the emotional cutoff concept was added by Bowen as the second last of the eight Family Systems Theory concepts.[16] The more we understand this seemingly mysterious concept of emotional cutoff, the greater opportunity we have to strengthen marriages.

The backdrop for Bowen's concept of emotional cutoff was the many young people running away from home during the 1960s. Parents were seen as the identified problem and getting away as the quick-fix solution. Bowen's assessment of the 1960s hippie movement's emotional cutoff from their parents rings true to us as children of the 1970s Jesus Movement. It may have looked to hippies as if they were being themselves and differentiating. More often they were still deeply attached and fused to their parents without realizing it. This was almost like the umbilical cord to their parents had never been cut.

Emotional cutoff is the extreme form of unresolved emotional distance. The term "distance" means in Latin "to stand apart." Chronic anxiety causes emotional distance to morph into emotional cutoff. We know many families, including our own, who have experienced multigenerational cutoff. The tragic early death of Ed's paternal grandmother Katherine Hird brought powerful multigenerational shock waves of emotional cutoff, including his grandfather Vic Hird's cutoff from God for many years until age 87. Part of Ed's fascination with emotional cutoff is because it is a strong multigenerational default within the Hird family system. He remembers being proud of this family pattern, which he participated in as a teenager. The phrase that they often tragically used was "I had to cut him off."

One of the reasons that there appears to be such a small Hird family is a result of being generationally cut off from many other Hird relatives. Great-Uncle Walter's daughter Helen Hird was emotionally cut off after she "got religion," married a born-again Christian, and went off to the Fraser Valley Bible Belt. We are still looking to reconnect with her and her family, wondering if she is living. One of our dreams is to find long-lost cousin Helen Hird and her children through the use of genealogical records as a way of bridging the generational Hird cutoff.

When people cannot remember when and why their ancestors left another country, it is often a clue to emotional cutoff from their families. Dr. Roberta Gilbert observed,

> America has sometimes been called a nation of cutoffs, since it was largely settled by immigrants.... It seems that the American way of growing up is to leave home and never return again, at least emotionally.[17]

Have you left home, resulting in cutoff from your family? Would you be interested in returning home emotionally? It can transform your marriage. Chronic anxiety causes emotional distance to morph into emotional cutoff. In our four-week Strengthening Marriage Workshop, we high-lighted four keys to bridging emotional cutoff.

CHAPTER 1

Digging for Marital Strengths

I n the first week of the Strengthening Marriage Workshop held in 2013, we focused on the first key to strengthening marriage by rediscovering strengths. Focusing primarily on a married couple's weaknesses tends to obscure their strengths and increases emotional cutoff.[18] The healing resources are already there inside the couple. They just need to be discovered and tapped into. Life is messy. Family is messy. Marriage is messy. How do we navigate through the complexities of married life? A key to healthy sailing through marriage's inevitable storms is gratitude for our spouse's often-hidden strengths.

Each of you reading this book is talented and gifted with many God-given abilities. Many people try to move forward in marriage by focusing primarily on their weaknesses: "This is what is wrong with our marriage. This is not good enough. We're not strong here." If you focus primarily on your weaknesses, you are rarely going to get to your future, because your weaknesses tend to make you feel hopeless. When you lose hope, you lose the future. Now, that doesn't mean that you ignore weaknesses. There are ways and times to deal with weaknesses, but when we are anxious, we put eighty to ninety percent of our focus on the weaknesses.

You remember when you were a teenager walking through the high school hallway? What were you sometimes feeling? Self-conscious? Panicked? *They're looking at me. They're staring at me. They can see my pimples. I am too tall, too short, too fat, too thin.* All of us have that inner teenager from time to time. As we focus on strengths, our anxiety level drops, and that is a huge key. When we are having challenges in our marriage, we don't naturally focus on strengths. We tend to ask, "What's wrong with you? You're not okay." Focusing on strengths is rarer than one might expect.[19] Ron Richardson commented,

I try to point out early in counseling the strengths every

couple displays in their lives. When they come for counseling, they often feel like failures. I make sure they know that I see the ways they are competent in life. This helps them put their difficulties in a larger perspective.[20]

In the Strengthening Marriage Workshop, Janice gave examples of Ed's strengths: "He is very fast, which is good and bad, but mostly good. He's great at doing the dishes and taking garbage out. He usually initially says no to requests, but as soon as he says no, he generally comes around and does what I ask him to do. So that's great. He will help with the meal preparation, which is really great. Ed will go ahead and do it. He is also very smart and interesting, because he is always wanting to grow and learn new things. I like that. He's very loving and kind as well. Ed likes to go for walks and other exercise. He is the athletic one in the family. But it is good for me, because I need to get out there and exercise. It is good that he encourages me."

Ed commented, "Janice's strengths are many. She is very affirmative. I'm a words-of-affirmation person. Janice is very gifted musically. We both love music, and that is a real strength that we enjoy together. Janice is very loving and caring. She is also a very good mother. She turns our house into a home. Janice has become a very good cook. We have three adult sons (and two daughters-in-law and two grandchildren now). So the family is expanding, and Janice is someone who loves to invest in family. She comes from the Prairies. Most prairie people like Janice are very family oriented with big families, compared to my side of the family. Janice is also very gifted administratively. She was once told that she has the spiritual gift of administration, which the person said, 'It probably sounds boring.' But it's very true."

So how do we grow together in marriage through our varying strengths? Ed has a strong leadership gifting and Janice has a strong administrative gifting. You can imagine that this would make us a good couple to organize a marriage workshop together. Janice will see the details that Ed won't. Ed has a gift of promoting, of getting the word out. Janice makes sure that we don't forget the details. When Ed is flexible with Janice's detailed requests, then it is a win-win."

We encourage you as a couple to try two strength-based exercises: a) I feel loved and appreciated when you…. b) I feel joyful when….

Here is what we said as a couple doing these two exercises:

Janice: "I feel loved and appreciated when Ed goes for walks with me. I feel joyful when he will share his latest ideas with me."

Ed: "I also feel loved and appreciated when Janice goes for a walk with me. I feel joyful when I see a couple holding hands and walking. I love to do this with Janice."

Clarity about each of our strengths brings greater clarity about our marriage. The most important thing in a healthy marriage is to be who you are. Many people have no sense of identity. They don't know who they are. Imagine if they could discover who they are, and then be it—for better, for worse. That could make a huge difference in a marriage—not trying to be someone else. Remember the peer pressure, especially when you were a teenager? It wasn't about being yourself, was it? It was more about being identical to everyone else. With emotional maturity, it becomes okay for you to be you and for your spouse to not be you and instead to be themselves.

Often you find your strengths and identity through some of the really painful things in your marriage. Have you ever found a strength in the midst of something really difficult?

One of Ed's most painful discoveries in Grade 10 was that he was not going to live out his seven-year-long dream of becoming an electrical engineer like his father. He was not mechanical or detailed enough. There was a sense of shame that he had disappointed his father. Ironically his dad never felt that way. But Ed had other strengths from his mother that enabled him to become a social worker and Anglican priest. Ed's mother was a natural-born counsellor with whom total strangers on city buses would share their life stories. It was pointless to lie to Ed's mother, as she was so intuitive. We will never forget what she first prophetically said to Janice: "The woman who marries Ed will need to carry quarters for the bus." Ed would often rush out to university without necessarily having change for the bus. Years later, with the birth of the Internet, Ed's engineering side became useful in helping to get the word out about his book to tens of thousands of social media followers. Ed is grateful that his father always cheered for him, even when he chose a different career path. Have either of your parents cheered for you, and encouraged your different strengths? Are you cheering for your spouse?

Dr. Paddy Ducklow said, "Cultivate in each other the courage to abandon ourselves to the wild ideas and heroic strengths of others (including your spouse)."[21] If we play marriage safe, it dies. Marriage is actually a potentially thrilling adventure based on strengths. For many people, adventure is not their strongest concept of marriage. Sometimes a masculine image of marriage is a ball and chain—"This is your last night of freedom"—not a symbol of adventure. When you think of some of the guy movies about weddings, they are often pushing the idea that marriage means your life is over. You are not told that you are entering an amazing adventure that will free you and liberate you. Too often we hear, "You've sown your wild oats. It's time to settle down and become responsible. You've had your fun. Now get on with being an adult." In Family Systems Theory, marriage is not meant to be just settling down. It's meant to be a wild, heroic adventure. God wants our hearts to be set on pilgrimage, on an amazing marital quest.[22] We invite you to talk with your spouse about how your marriage could be more of an adventure. Dr. E. Stanley Jones said,

> Many live in dread of what is coming. Why should we? The unknown puts adventure into life....The unexpected around the corner gives a sense of anticipation and surprise. Thank God for the unknown future.[23]

One of the wildest adventures that we have experienced was going to the former pirate island of Crete, where Ed wrote the book *Restoring Health: Body, mind and spirit.* The island of Crete had been swarming with pirates since at least the 8th century BC.[24] Errol Flynn or Johnny Depp, who played the charmingly deceptive Captain Jack Sparrow in the movie series *Pirates of the Caribbean,* would have been right at home in ancient Crete. All Cretans, according to their own prophet Epimenides, were liars, evil brutes, and lazy gluttons.[25] In other words, they were pirates and proud of it. Titus, the focus of Ed's book, taught toxic Cretan pirates how to become radically healthy ex-pirates: how to love, how to lay down their lives for another, how to be the faithful husband of but one wife, how to be gentle and patient.

While there, we took time to view Titus's preserved head, which the Venetians returned to the Hagio Tito church in Crete in 1966. We found the Cretan people very hospitable, especially Fr. Makarios Grinezakis, the official preacher for the Orthodox Church of Crete. Because Greek, and indeed European, civilization can be traced back to Crete, there are reportedly over 2,000 scholars and archeologists on Crete.[26] The food, culture, and music are very soothing and captivating, reflecting the beauty of Crete and the unbreakable spirit of its people. We will never forget our amazing Cretan adventure.

How can couples move into their daring adventure, their preferred marital future? We move forward by building on what is already working. This is not about getting stuck in the past; rather it is about valuing the existing strengths that you each bring to your relationship. Marriage is about risking together. Many people leave their marriage because the risk dies. Everything's predictable. Everything's the same. Everything's about safety, and safety kills. It's boring. It is not really that our spouse is boring but that we have negotiated ourselves into this tiny little version of a marriage. Every time we feel anxious, we are tempted to shrink our marriage. If you keep shrinking your marriage down to feeling safe, it becomes tinier and tinier and tinier. The adventure completely disappears. Would you like to start risking again, for better, for worse?

Part of our marital adventure is to write books and to go on ministry trips. Janice thought she was going to speak for fifteen to twenty minutes at a Christian Ashram retreat that we were at in Ontario. They wanted her to speak for an hour about her life. She had never spoken anywhere for an hour. Speaking was Ed's strength. What Janice liked to do was sing. When we arrived, they wanted Janice to speak for a second hour the next day. Janice thought, *Two hours! I can't do that. Okay, I will have to sing some music then.* So she sang *Because He Lives,* and they sang with her, and that was easier. Janice discovered that the retreat participants really enjoyed her talks. She has never been the same.

Our 2011 mission trip to Rwanda that same summer was very

exciting. We were able to meet some Rwandan teenagers who were eager to learn songs in English. Ed videotaped it all and put it up on YouTube. It was so much fun. We also did a marriage workshop with Rwandan couples engaged to be married. They were so pleased with the teaching that they wanted us to stay and come to their weddings. We were able to use our strengths, both known and previously hidden, on these mission adventures. What, perhaps hidden, strengths might launch you and your spouse on a "for better, for worse" adventure?

CHAPTER 2

Celebrating Our Differences

The focus of the second week of our Strengthening Marriage Workshop was strengthening marriage through celebrating differences. Self-differentiation in marriage honours differences and otherness. You may remember the immortal line by Dr. Henry Higgins from the musical *My Fair Lady*: "Why can't a woman be more like a man?" Emotional fusion, the loss of one's identity, demands marital sameness. Yet being identical is the enemy of true identity, particularly in marriage.

Before we were married, we would meet on the bus and talk on the way to university. We would discuss the Bible and, even though we would not always agree, Janice would pretend that she did. It was a few years later that she admitted this. She was using what Family Systems Theory calls the pseudo-self. When a husband is most calmly differentiated, he revels in his wife's otherness. While a wife's pseudo-self can temporarily pretend to be the same as her husband's self, her core self is radically and uniquely not the same as her husband's. Ed and Janice have been learning how to remove their masks and revel in each other's uniquenesses. Do you enjoy how different your spouse is from you?

Janice sometimes likes to stay up late. Early risers, like Ed, often fall asleep when watching movies at night. He ironically remembers coaching a couple where the wife did not feel loved because her husband would sometimes nod off during evening TV shows. One of the most well-known couples in the world are Nicky and Pippa Gumbel of Holy Trinity Brompton in London. Over thirty-million people around the world have taken their amazing Alpha Course.[27] On the Alpha Course, Nicky humorously related how people knew that he would marry Pippa, because for the first time in his life, while dating her, he stayed up past 9pm. It has taken time for Ed and Janice to rejoice in each other's different time clocks.

The heart of the word *differentiation* is the word *difference*. Working on one's own self is the key to raising the level of differentiation in the marriage. When people get married, they become one, but they are not always sure which one. What people underestimate when they get married is how much they get swallowed by their well-meaning spouse and how much they lose identity. We are still working on this tendency forty years into our marriage. People are tempted to either give away self to the other spouse or take self from the other spouse. Dominant people have a tendency to take self from the other partner. Less dominant and more compliant people will often give away self to the other partner. Do you tend to be more of a taker or giver of self in your marriage? What was your parents' pattern in giving and taking self in their marriage? Was one parent more dominant?

Bowen called self-differentiation the principal subject and the cornerstone of Family Systems Theory. No other concept is so often discussed and associated with Bowen's work.[28] The concept of self-differentiation is "generally the most difficult one for people to grasp and apply."[29] One of the challenges to this very important Bowenian concept is that it is very different, quite unintelligible to many people. Their eyes often glaze over when we first use the term. *Differentiation* is not even found as a noun in some dictionaries. The closest term in the *Concise Oxford Dictionary* is the verb *differentiate*, which is helpfully defined as "constitute the difference between; develop into unlikeness, specialize, discriminate between (from the noun *difference* [Latin: differentia])." To become adult in one's marriage is to specialize, to become different and unique. The beauty of one's spouse is that they are not us. Can you think of one positive way that your spouse is not like you? Are you willing to share this with them?

Self-differentiation helps us think more clearly. Thinking helps us have a better marriage. Richardson said that "in matters involving romantic love, it is particularly important to be able to think."[30] Some people believe that thinking and romantic love do not mix. Thoughtfulness actually increases romantic love. How thoughtful are you in loving and cherishing your spouse? As thinking increases, anxiety decreases. Richardson also said that "what many people often mean by 'closeness' is actually 'sameness' in thinking, feeling and behaviour…. Pushing for sameness causes distancers to distance more."[31] How much room does your family give you to celebrate diversity and differences, in contrast to pushing for sameness?

The heart of Family Systems Theory is clear thinking, sometimes called "thinking systems" or "thinking in systems."[32] Bowen had the ability to "think in motion."[33] Family Systems Theory is about the big picture. Thinking in systems is a learned skill that does not come naturally for many people. Sometimes the intense chaos of marital relations leads people to believe that there are no patterns and no order to be found. Bowen was one researcher who was able to take this step back and to discover that there was indeed an order and predictability in what he called a seemingly impenetrable thicket.

As a former Freudian psychoanalyst, Bowen birthed most of his Family Systems Theory concepts in the midst of his disappointment with the relative ineffectiveness of Freudian counselling. Self-awareness and new information, while important, do not by themselves bring transformation in married couples. Bowen was also concerned about the tendency of Freudianism to blame the parents. Family Systems Theory seeks to blame no one.[34] What if we gave up blaming our parents and spouse and sought to see them with new eyes? What is important to hear and see, said Bowen, is not what is in people but what is in between people. Bowen was one of those rare individuals with "a genuinely new idea."[35] As many of Bowen's students were ex-Freudians, they "literally had to untrain themselves … from individual concepts in order to see the family emotional system."[36] Bowen became to many an ex-Freudian heretic, leading Friedman to comment that "Bowen theory is often so anathema to many therapists that it isn't even mentioned."[37] In many circles, Bowen Theory is treated if it doesn't exist.

Bowen developed the concept of self-differentiation through observing how feelings and intellect were either fused or distinguished from each other. Differentiation is the opposite of emotional fusion. People who have trouble being different get swallowed by their problematic relationships.[38] Having a high IQ is no guarantee of emotional intelligence.[39]

The term *differentiation*, said Bowen, was chosen because of its specific meanings in the biological sciences. Bowen's theory involves two opposing basic life forces. One is a built-in life growth force toward individuality and the differentiation of a separate "self," and the other is an equally intense emotional closeness.[40]

Bowen saw differentiation as equivalent to one's identity and individuality.[41] It is worth asking, Who am I really? We are much more than our work or our education. By strengthening our sense of self and personal identity, we strengthen our marriage. How much attention have you or your spouse given to strengthening your personal identity? Is that a new way of thinking about marriage for you? Our highest identity as believers is found in Christ through the Spirit of adoption. This may seem rather abstract initially, but it can be radically life changing. Your work, education, or bank account will no longer ultimately define you. A marriage can be radically strengthened when we realize that we are sons or daughters of the Almighty God. This is our truest identity. Everything else is temporary. Did you know that God is waiting to adopt you for now and eternity?[42]

Getting married can unexpectedly bring with it a major loss of self. In the closeness of an intense relationship, the emotional selves blend, or fuse together, into a common self, a "we-ness."[43] Such togetherness, "we-ness," is uncomfortable for the couple. So they may use sameness as an anxiety reducer.[44] Richardson said that "most people get married thinking their spouse is like them…. When differences emerge, most of us try to make our partner more like them."[45] Anyone ever done that? Janice and Ed have certainly tried that. We have no idea how radically different we are. This we-ness almost automatically leads to conflict. The paradox of differentiation is that it opens the space for true togetherness, how to get both closer and yet more distinct. Each spouse can enjoy the full spectrum of emotional closeness without giving up self.[46] In the Strengthening Marriage Workshop, we taught about differentiation, saying,

> Being different is not just okay, it is wonderful. The challenge
> is to learn to celebrate these differences. It is part of the reason

that you married each other, because you weren't the same. If you are both identical, one of you is unnecessary. Would you like to be married to yourself? [[chuckles]] What would it be like being married to yourself? [[comments by participants: Boring. Unnecessary. Terrible.] The exciting thing about otherness is that, while it can be painful, it is one of the exciting keys to growth. We need to celebrate the otherness of our spouse and actually value it. It has been said that we marry people because they are different, and then we spend much time fussing and trying to change them to be like us. Is it okay for you to be you? Sometimes it doesn't feel like it is. Often, we don't even know who we are.[47]

"'We-ness' is undifferentiation, or fusion, which will bring about three dysfunctions in couples: (1) marital conflict, (2) symptoms in a spouse, including sickness, or (3) dysfunction in their child."[48] These three dysfunctions are primary "reasons" for married couples seeking counselling.[49] Defining self is life-giving and foundational. Differentiation, said Bowen, deals with working on one's self, with controlling self, with becoming a more responsible person, and with permitting others to be themselves.[50] Is it okay in your marriage for you and your spouse to be yourselves?

Differentiation of self is a lifelong process that involves knowing the boundaries of where your self begins and ends.[51] Learning to say no and to set healthy boundaries strengthens marital intimacy. Many people are starving for authentic connection with their spouse. Better boundaries allow people to connect with their spouse openly, equally, and with self-definition.[52] Through boundaries, spouses are able to stay in touch when tempted to distance. The healthiest boundaries are secure but permeable. What do your boundaries look like in your marriage?

When any of our three sons is in crisis, our boundaries get challenged. We will do anything for them, sometimes too much. When both parents are overachievers, it can be hard for children to grow up and stand on their own two feet. Reggie McNeal says that "an inability to say no reflects a boundary problem.... [They] are afraid that that people will abandon them if they do not yield to other's demands, or afraid that people will quit liking them."[53] Do you find it hard to say no to your spouse, to your family? As women were coming into a greater awareness, you may remember the expressions "*No* means *no*" and "What part of ***no*** do you not understand?" For many women in numerous cultures, saying no was hugely difficult and very countercultural. Did you have the permission in your family to say no? Saying no gives you the ability to say yes. Self-differentiating is about thoughtfully choosing both your *yeses* and your *nos*. Many people nowadays are very workaholic and overfunctioning. They say yes to too many things. Driving their children everywhere to endless activities leaves them exhausted. Without boundaries, there is nothing left for your marriage. Research shows that exhaustion and physical intimacy are opposites.[54] It is too easy in marriage to be sexually selfish and insensitive to our spouse's sexual needs. What if we became more generous to our spouse? Sometimes generosity is noticing how exhausted your spouse is and perhaps intentionally non-sexually touching them gently without expecting it to go to the bedroom. How exhausting has life been for you or your spouse recently?

No one likes being neglected by their spouse. It is too easy in this 24/7 culture to unintentionally ignore our spouse's needs. Because opposites attract, your spouse's needs are likely very different than yours, and that is great. The more differentiated we are, the less that we unwisely try to fix our spouse and make them just like us. Love, says Dr. Gil Stieglitz, is meeting needs, pursuing your spouse's soul, and seeking to please.[55] Do you know what your spouse's top needs are? Wives, says Stieglitz, want to know on a daily basis that they are number one in our lives (under God), ahead of our work, sports, family, and other activities. Otherwise they will feel dishonoured and not valued. If a husband does not daily honour his wife, she will not be able to emotionally and physically respond to him. The Good Book even teaches that a husband's prayers will not be answered if he consistently dishonours his wife.[56] Problems frequently arise when one's spouse does something hurtful, then promises never to do it again but keeps breaking that promise. We have seen much grief among the people to whom we minister when spouses put their work or their children first, merely giving each other the leftovers. Both quality and quantity time are the gift of covenant love. How might you covenant to give more of your precious time to your beloved? Time is love. To love and to cherish may mean putting your spouse back into your busy schedule, intentionally blocking off uninterrupted time with them.

Clergy, too, can easily be overwhelmed by the endless demands on their time and requests for help from other people. It doesn't matter how long and hard you work serving people as a pastor; someone will often be unhappy and want more from you. Ed has had to learn to be intentional in making time to be with his beloved Janice. Time with her busy pastor father was both precious and too rare. It left wounds. Because Janice is Ed's best friend, he has learned to put Janice ahead of the endless demands of ministry. We do that by setting specific appointments in our schedules to reconnect with each other through going for walks or dinner dates. Healthy boundaries don't happen by accident. Sadly, many husbands stop dating their wives after they marry. Many wives wonder, "What happened to the man I married? Why was he so attentive before marriage, and now he would rather hang out on the golf course or stay late at work?" Our wives deeply need to be romanced, pursued, won over every week. What might weekly dating look like in your current or future marriage?

While male friends are often happy with side-by-side conversations, women usually want face-to-face interaction. Your wife wants your undivided attention. Part of Ed and Janice falling in love was their singing together. Janice would never have married a non-singer. Ed's ability to sing has unexpectedly returned, which is thrilling to both of us. He even sang again in the St. Simon's Christmas concert. Recently Ed and Janice were having a wonderful private music practice together when suddenly a text came through on his cell phone. Unwisely he quickly read the text, leaving Janice feeling dishonoured and ignored. Ed apologized, and thankfully she forgave him. It grieved Ed that he hurt Janice in this way. How do you and your spouse keep your cell phone from stealing your couple time? What might need to change?

Friedman said that "the problem is how to preserve self in close relationships. That's the critical issue."[57] To some married couples, self-defining may seem counterintuitive. We think we already know

everything about our spouse. Part of self-defining
share our true self with our spouse.[58] Higher-dif
less needy and therefore less threatened when '
new aspect of their personality. For some cou
is like a "drug" without which they cannot '
couples learn to value time apart as well as time to
been like for you to spend time apart from your spouse?

Being your own person reduces chronic anxiety. Being yourself
is more attractive than lacking identity. It takes only one person to
make a change for the better. One spouse will make the first move as
they begin to negotiate a brand-new marriage.[59] If the differentiating
spouse can maintain their position without attacking or distancing,
the marriage will get a breakthrough.[60]

There is no perfect marriage. Rejecting perfectionism is key to a
healthier marriage. Friedman noted, "In reality, no human marriage
gets a rating of more than 70%."[61] Reaching seventy in the self-differentiation scale is the new 100. We encourage you to stop being so
hard on yourselves. How might you show more grace and kindness
to your imperfect spouse and to your imperfect self, for better, for
worse?

Janice tends to be perfectionistic, having trained at the UBC
School of Music. Every musical note or word had to be sung a certain
way. One of her highest compliments, when she was first married,
would be to say "not bad." Ed, feeling insecure, didn't find that very
encouraging. Many years later, Janice had a dream that she saw an
angel lying in mid-air beside her as she and Ed were sleeping. The
angel was the length of the room and was in gold-plated armour.
Janice said to the angel, "Do you have something important to tell
me?" The angel said to her, "Yes, be kind to your husband." The angel
then disappeared. Janice knew that it had to be from God because she
would have never dreamed those words up by herself. So she tried to
be kinder and more loving to her imperfect husband.

Married couples often prefer "business as usual" compared to the
risks of redefining their precarious relationship.[62] Bowen taught,

> Differentiation begins when one family member begins to
> more clearly define and openly state his own inner life princi-

and convictions, and he begins to take responsible action based on convictions.... The remainder of the family opposes this differentiating effort with a powerful emotional counter-force, which goes in successive steps: (1) "You are wrong" with volumes of reasons to support this; (2) "Change back and we will accept you again"; and (3) "If you don't, these are the consequences," which are then listed.[63]

Self-differentiation is already inside of the married couple, waiting to be drawn out through thoughtful listening to each other's hopes and challenges. Like Ed's late mother, Janice is a great listener. Ed can share anything with her. The more we understand our self, the more we understand our spouse. The Good Book says that husbands are to live with their wife in an understanding way, something that some husbands think is impossible.[64] Self-differentiation requires great courage. One of the terms in Family Systems Theory is *self-regulating,* or calming yourself down. Sometimes you need to say, "I need to go to the gym" or "I need to go for a walk." It can be helpful to set a time so that you are not gone indefinitely: "I will be gone for an hour or two before I come back." Men often need some down time before they can continue discussing relationally intense subjects.

What key principles guide your marriage? How principled are you? The term *principle* comes from the Latin word *princeps,* meaning "first, chief." What comes first for you in your marriage? Self-differentiation is based on well-thought-through guiding principles, which are inherently calming for married couples. Such principles are not held rigidly but are open to new data. Marital openness is the opposite of marital cutoff. Openness to one's parents is the foundation of marital open-ness.[65] If we cut our parents off, we are more likely to cut our spouse off. Guiding principles help us discover and mature our basic self as opposed to our pseudo-self. These principles are not uncovered easily and quickly but rather through thinking, investigating, testing, and retesting. What might be one of your key relationship principles?

One of the key principles for Janice is Ed coming home on time. Many years ago, before cell phones, Ed was visiting a couple who were close to a major breakthrough in their lives. When Ed finally returned home very late, Janice could not share in Ed's joy over this breakthrough. He had neglected to phone her and let her know when he would be coming home. So Janice was worried that he might have been in a car accident. After this painful night, he promised to phone her if he would be later than ten o'clock.

One of Ed's key principles is quality time with Janice. When the children were young, this was more difficult. Janice was raised in a family that never stopped, didn't have many boundaries, and thought that children's needs always came first. Sometimes Ed would feel ignored and lonely. Has this scenario ever happened in your family? Janice learned that if she made time for Ed, then everyone in the family benefited, including the children.

Does your family ever wear masks? The pseudo-self, the mask that we wear to protect ourselves, is where many of us live most of the time.[66] Bowen said that

> differentiation begins when one family member begins to more clearly define and openly state his own life principles and convictions, and he begins to take responsible action based on convictions.[67]

Our family has gone through our share of difficulties, but because we stand together, our marriage has made it through all the hard times, for better, for worse. Because we stand together, we have greater courage to take sometimes unpopular stands, even for biblical marriage. Who might have imagined that standing for biblical marriage might one day become controversial? Daring to be different, taking principled stands, having clear goals—all these things strengthen marriage. Many people are afraid to do this in their marriage. They are fearful to take a stand because their spouse might leave them, they might push back, and there might be sabotage. Any time you do take a stand, there will possibly be sabotage, if not from your spouse, then probably someone in your family. That is just part of the turf. Being a people-pleaser, bending yourself into a pretzel, giving up self harms your marriage. Richardson says that "many a husband and wife have failed to take a principled stand in their marriage simply because they feared the loss of their partnership if they did."[68] The worry is that their spouse will walk away, so spouses think that they have to conform or shut themselves down. Have you ever bent yourself into a pretzel trying to please others? We both have. It doesn't work.

Having principles in marriage does not mean being rigid. The term *rigid* comes from the Latin word *rigidus,* meaning "unable to bend, stiff, inflexible, not able to change, not adaptable." The more rigid we are, the more vulnerable we are to loss of self and/or loss of our marriage. Rigidity is emotional death, often resulting in marital death. Principles are best held flexibly. It is about knowing who you are and what is important to you. This can include negotiation. Richardson also says that "typically the goal-oriented person has quite good, meaningful and close relationships and encounters fewer problems in maintaining intimate relationships."[69] Many spouses are unaware that greater clarity about their personal goals and principles brings better sexual intimacy. The term *intimate* comes from the Latin word *intimus*, meaning *innermost*. We encourage you to be clear about your innermost goals, your direction for your marriage, who you are and where you are heading. Many people don't have goals. How might working on your goals help your marriage? Can you identify any innermost goals that you have for your marriage? Have you ever shared them with your spouse?

One of Ed and Janice's mutual goals and principles is to be healthier. We have spent many hours discussing ways to embrace a more healthy lifestyle. This has included going to the gym, cutting out gluten and dairy, reducing our intake of sugar and salt, going for regular walks, playing with our grandchildren at the park, and swimming at the local pool. This mutual interest resulted in Ed's latest book, *Restoring Health: body, mind and spirit.*[70] Since Ed's successful stent surgery in 2017, we are even more motivated to live out these healthy principles, for better, for worse.

If we do not speak up, we lose identity and self-awareness of our thinking and core convictions. "All you need is love," sang the Beatles. There is a temptation to believe the myth that being loving and kind by itself will cure all of our marriage conflicts. Love is sometimes confused with giving up self. True love self-differentiates. If we do not speak up to our spouse, we lose identity, self, and self-awareness of our thinking and core convictions. One way to speak up is through learning to use "I" statements. Using "I" statements helps us focus on core principles and thoughtful courses of actions. Is it normal to use "I" statements in your family? Learning to use "I" statements as a married couple takes time. It is often our families that resist such self-definition.[71] When a spouse uses "I" statements rather than just "we" statements, it helps them take responsibility for their own growth and health. Through self-defining "I" statements, a spouse avoids blaming or taking responsibility for the other spouse's emotions and actions. Bowen called such an "I" position "doing what you say and saying what you do."[72] Highly fused spouses do "I" statements narcissistically, saying only "I want, I hurt." Self-differentiated spouses will say "I am… I believe… I will do… I will not do."[73] Would you like to experiment with doing an "I" statement with your spouse? Remember to be gentle, particularly if this way of differentiating is unfamiliar to your spouse.

It may have been normal in your family to make "you" statements when angry. Did your family ever say "You always do…" or "You never do…"? What if you tried saying "I find it painful when…" or "I need to have time to…" or "I need a hug?" In both Janice and Ed's families, "you" statements were more common than "I" statements.

When we first married, we had both previously learned to blame other people, especially each other, when pressured. We might say phrases like "Why did you do that?" or "You always do that." Through retraining ourselves to use "I " statements, we greatly reduced our tendency to blame each other. Instead we started saying phrases like "I don't like it when you leave your dirty socks on the floor" or "I am uncomfortable when you drive so fast." Even though we know better, it is still tempting at times to slip back into the old familiar blaming behaviours.

People with low differentiation often default to emotional distance and marital cutoff as their anxiety reducer. Bowen spoke about lower-differentiated people acting like relational nomads, going from marriage to marriage and then to short-term relationships.[74] When differentiation is higher, one can be fully involved in one's marriage without fear of becoming too fused. Most higher-differentiated people are still affected by anxiety but recover more quickly. Higher differentiation in couples enables more flexible change.[75] How open are you to change in your marriage relationship, for better, for worse?

Differentiation for married couples is about becoming more intimate.[76] Have you or your spouse ever lost interest in each other? Has the original fire that drew you together ever waned? Are you longing for more romance in your marriage? Emotional and sexual boredom is often a sign of rigid, fused undifferentiation. Such fused couples are often both addictively drawn to each other and simultaneously drawn to flee from each other.[77] The lower the differentiation, the more likely that one spouse will become more dominant, taking self from the other more compliant one, who gives up self.[78] The more compliant we are, the less energy and creativity we have for lasting transformation. Marriage relationships, which all have a tendency to deteriorate if neglected, decline more quickly and dramatically when self-differentiation is low.[79]

Humour, unlike sarcasm, helps us differentiate. It is part of a healthy marriage. In the Hird family system, sarcasm was normal. One day, one of Ed's sisters said to him, "I have been convicted lately about sarcasm. I have decided to stop being sarcastic." Ed was thinking "Good for you," and then he thought, "Me too." Sarcasm can rip you apart and shred you. Ed realized that it was a family issue, so he decided to swear off sarcasm. This is easier said than done. Giving up sarcasm doesn't, however, mean giving up humour. How does humour play out in your marriage? Appropriate humour actually reduces tension almost like it pops a balloon. Janice's family has a wonderful humorous laugh. Humour, which sometimes includes irony and a sense of the tragicomic, is a key strategy in self-differentiation for married couples. When spouses don't know how to de-stress, it leaves them vulnerable to self-medication. Humour reduces fusion in marriages.[80] Often a casual comment with light humour can do wonders. Have you ever found humour helpful in dealing with relational conflict?

At the heart of self-differentiation in one's marriage is a non-anxious presence. Some married couples slip back and forth from an anxious presence to an anxious non-presence. Have you ever wondered where your spouse disappeared to? Through avoidance, substance abuse, or workaholism, some spouses temporarily achieve a non-anxious absence.[81] What we desire is presence, being present to oneself, one's marriage, one's family, and others. Being present without being swallowed is the key. It is so easy to not "be there." Bowen became so emphatic about this insight that he became known as Dr. Presence.[82] How present are you in your marriage? Have you checked out? Did your spouse notice when you were non-present? All of us can be tempted to be absent both from our spouse and even God: "Where can I flee from your presence?"[83]

In Janice's family, they were all supposed to be the same. Everyone was supposed to work hard. Her mother would say, "Janice, you can work and talk at the same time." Sometimes as a child, Janice would go off and hide so that she wouldn't have to work. Her mother was very controlling and overwhelming, so Janice used to hide from her mother. Her mom wasn't trying to be mean; she was just overwhelming. She never beat Janice or anything. Her mother wanted to know everything about Janice; but Janice wouldn't share with her. Janice didn't really know how to self-differentiate from her mother. Then she met Ed and was glad to get out of the house through marriage.

Janice's mom found Ed before Janice did. By God-incidence, her mother and Ed met each other at a 1974 weekend interdenominational conference in Squamish, BC. Despite his longish hair and embroidered overalls, Ed made quite an impression on Janice's mother, Vera. She had really enjoyed a movie that was popular at the time, *Fiddler on the Roof*, and she could sing one of its hit songs by heart: "Matchmaker, Matchmaker, make me a match, Find me a find, catch me a catch…"

Unfortunately, when Ed's future mother-in-law/matchmaker commended him to her daughter, the assessment was not mutual. Janice and Ed had attended the same high school in Grade 12—and we all know that familiarity can breed contempt. Janice didn't want her mother controlling her relationships. They met again a few years later at the University of British Columbia. Janice was attracted to Ed for a year, but he didn't notice. He just saw her as a good friend, a phase in relationships that is key to a healthy marriage. Have you noticed how many romances start in the spring? One day in May, Ed invited Janice out bike riding. Something clicked. On the second bike ride, Ed said to her, "Don't take me too seriously, but relative to two days, I'd like to spend the rest of my life with you." Janice felt overwhelmed by this comment, and said "I just broke up with my fiancé and am not ready to get serious." Two years later they tied the knot in holy matrimony.

Janice's mother phoned her often, even though Janice was now married, and she would be hurt if Janice didn't phone her back immediately. Her mom was overwhelming, and Janice didn't know how to self-differentiate from her mom. But often, of course, people marry someone who is like someone in their family. Janice married Ed. Like her mother, he is very affectionate and loving; but, especially the first year, he was quite overwhelming. Janice was a middle child, so she always tried to get along. She did what he wanted, even though she gave up self in the process. Janice found it hard that first year, having someone in her space all the time, because we lived in a one-room apartment. She was used to having more room, but we survived. Ed didn't mean to be controlling. He was just overwhelming, like Janice's mom.

One of the unintended consequences of emotional cutoff is increased loss of self. To give up one's genuine self is to cease to be. When cutoffs occur in marriage, both people always lose something of themselves. People who are cut off from their families generally do not heal until they have been reconnected. How cut off are you from your parents and family? Have you ever tried to reconnect? What was that like for you?

If you emotionally fuse with your spouse, you will lose your core identity and become more anxious. Sometimes Ed has given up self to Janice when he is driving; her desire to be helpful can leave Ed feeling controlled. For some reason, controlling people don't like being controlled by others. Ed has said to Janice, "Would you rather drive?" Though outwardly quieter, Janice can sometimes, when anxious, be overwhelming and controlling like her mom. People who take self from others don't like having self taken from themselves. They don't usually like a taste of their own medicine. Ed was also fused to his family. At Ed's family dinner table, he was rarely able to finish a sentence without others completing it or changing the topic. He later learned to respond to interruptions by just stopping in midsentence and waiting. After a while, his family members would say, "Ed, why didn't you finish what you were saying?"

Married couples use emotional distance as an avoidance of their own fusion to each other. Nagging one's spouse over their distancing behaviour just drives them further away. Distance serves as an emotional insulator, almost like a cocoon.[84] Emotional distance is a high price for tense peace. Much marital conflict is ironically fostered by attempts to avoid it. Another thing that Ed discovered while working on his doctorate is that he is a conflict avoider. People who are conflict avoiders often marry the other expression, people who will actually pursue them. The problem with conflict avoidance is that it doesn't work. Ed started noticing himself avoid conflict. His fantasy would be a marriage in which Janice and Ed always got along and never disagreed. But there is no such world—and it would not even be healthy.

CHAPTER 3

The Joy of Conflict

The theme of the third week of the Strengthening Marriage Workshop was strengthening marriages through valuing conflict. Did anyone ever tell you, when you got married, that conflict would be a key to a better marriage? We often think that conflict is a sign of a bad marriage, but it isn't. There are no conflict-free marriages. Whether it's about wanting more physical intimacy, facing the piling-up laundry, seeing the in-laws, or paying monthly bills, conflict is inevitable in every marriage. So we need to reframe conflict as something that is healthy and a key to breakthrough. How many of you want a breakthrough in your marriage? Conflict is one of the keys, for better, for worse.

We all want deeper intimacy. What in the world is deeper intimacy? What does it look like? The irony is that intimacy comes through facing conflict. We often deal with conflict the same way our parents did. You may vow "I'll never be like my dad or mom." But unless you deal with it, you will repeat the past in your new relationship. The good news is that you can make shifts. Part of the shift is dropping judgments, blame, and criticism. In this way, conflict actually brings lasting change. To really change is to become different, more differentiated. You can bring short-term change, but a lot of it just recycles. Very little change lasts. We can all change for a day or two, can't we? But it doesn't last. Don't we all want lasting change? Some people just give up. They say "I'm stuck. I can't change. My spouse will never change. My parents will never change."

Some psychological researchers are primarily measuring symptomatic change rather than the more significant long-term change.[85] As such, the marital research results may be misleading, as it takes years to bring lasting systemic change in one's marriage.[86] In western society, we want fast results. Quick symptomatic relief of anxiety is not the same as long-term marital change. Friedman commented,

> Much, if not most, of the change that occurs in families

and other institutions does not last. And much of what we thought was change often recycles either in a different form or in a different location.[87]

What temporary change has recycled in your marriage and family? Whom do we try to change? It is often our spouse, which is basically an entire waste of time, isn't it? You know the Serenity Prayer: "God grant me the serenity to accept the things that I cannot change [which is anyone or anything else], the courage to change the things I can [which is yourself], and the wisdom to know the difference." That is hard work. Lasting change comes through working on self. It is often the last thing that anyone wants to do. Only lasting personal change can bring a lasting, satisfying marriage. That is what this marriage book is all about.

Bowen emphatically said that one of the greatest diseases of humanity is to try to change a fellow human being.[88] Our futile attempt to change our spouse indicates self-serving nonacceptance, which will likely be resisted on principle. The more that we push our spouse to change, the more likely is marital and emotional cutoff. The more differentiated we are, the less urgent is this desire to change our spouse. It is incredibly liberating to be freed from the "need" to change one's spouse. Bowen taught that it is never really possible to change another person, but it is possible to change the part that self plays.[89] What if you gave up trying to change your spouse, and instead gave them over to God? Is that too shocking of an idea for you?

One of our sons had gone to Mexico on a mission trip in the summer before Grade 11. When he came back, he wasn't feeling well. It turned out that he had picked up three kinds of parasites. The worst one they didn't find for three months. Every morning he would vomit. Because he didn't feel well, he wouldn't want to go to school. At the same time, he was in the *Joseph* musical. So, we became quite upset that he didn't want to go to school while still singing in the musical. Then he started to feel better, but he still didn't want to go to school because he was depressed from being sick. Janice told Ed that he would have to deal with this crisis. Ed was very conflicted and upset about it. We were in such desperate straits that we all went and talked to a counsellor. The counsellor's daughter was a tutor, so she helped our son get through the twenty assignments in which he was behind. It was hard, but it was really good for our family because we learned to deal with conflict in a more productive way instead of a negative way. If you do it right, making up after conflict results in an unexpectedly stronger relationship.

Janice and Ed are avid readers. But we read books in different ways, which can unexpectedly lead to conflict. When Ed reads a book, he loves to share. But sharing usually means interrupting Janice's reading of her own book. Because she's very kind, she puts up with this before going back to her mystery novel. So we have had conflict over this seemingly minor issue many times in our forty years of marriage. We usually have conflict every other day, but we get over it quickly and forgive each other. If it is something that Janice is really upset with, it might take her a few hours, but usually it is only a couple of minutes to get over it. It's not worth it to stay stuck in your anger. You may have heard the phrase "If Mama ain't happy, ain't nobody happy." When we were first married, Janice used to get upset because Ed wouldn't roll up the toothpaste tube nicely the way she was taught to do it. She eventually realized it was nothing to keep getting upset about. Janice and Ed have made up and forgiven each other thousands of times in the past forty years.

One of the signs of marital cutoff is strong resistance to change. To be homeostatic in one's marriage is to have a strong default to "business as usual," even when it is toxic. Our attempts to change often fall flat. The good news is that by valuing and observing our initial failures to change, we are more likely to experience lasting marital change. Even failures can be used in the marital adventure. How willing are you to radically change in your marriage? How homeostatic and resistant to change were your parents in their marriage? How willing are you to get out of the boat and walk on water with your spouse?

You may remember that we saved money to visit Israel and Europe in 1980. In Israel we visited all the places where Jesus walked, including the Sea of Galilee. We also tried to walk on water. It didn't work at the Sea of Galilee, but it almost worked at the Dead Sea, where we were able to read a newspaper while floating on our backs. We deeply fell in love with the land and people of Israel. Janice also enjoyed going to Austria, where one of her favourite composers, Mozart, was born. We also loved visiting Italy, France, Germany, and especially Great Britain, where we both still had living relatives to visit. Even though our saving for this trip was done awkwardly, we are grateful that we took a risk and had this unforgettable adventure on our third anniversary.

Herbert Otto, in the book *Marriage and Family Enrichment,* said that "conflict is but the agony of a marriage being born, not a symptom of sickness. Just as in all birth processes, there are labour pains."[90] For the rest of your life, your marriage is continually being birthed through different conflicts with your spouse. Have you had any labour pains in your marriage? Labour pains in marriage are actually healthy. When you are in the middle of conflict, it is very painful. If we could go from being conflict-phobic to being conflict-friendly in our marriages, that would bring a breakthrough. Dr. John Gottman discovered that 69 percent of relational conflict is unsolvable. This perpetual conflict is best managed through working on what Gottman calls the Four Horsemen: criticism, contempt, stonewalling, and defensiveness. He found that 85 percent of stonewallers are men. When their heart rate goes over 100, stonewallers are most likely to give their spouse the silent treatment. Gottman has found that the Four Horsemen can accurately predict the likelihood of divorce 94 percent of the time.[91] What helps you de-escalate from the Four Horsemen of criticism, contempt, stonewalling, and defensiveness? Do you ever use planned "time outs" for an hour or so when your emotions are flooded during conflict? Gottman says that how we make up is even more important than how we do conflict.[92] How do you and your partner make up after conflict? Do you remember how your parents made up? Or were your parents' times of conflict and making up hidden from you? How might you like to change your pattern of making up?

Married couples often suffer from a repeating pattern of too much closeness and too much distance. Bowen called it a "closeness–fighting-rejecting cycle."[93] The rejected often reject others. Being close can be very demanding. Distance is often vital in preserving the pseudo-self. If taken too far, distance can feel like abandonment. Kerr and Bowen commented that

> a hallmark of a conflictual marriage is that husband and wife are angry and dissatisfied with one another.... Their relationship is like an exhausting, draining, and strangely invigorating roller coaster ride; people threaten never to buy another ticket, but they usually do.[94]

Have you ever had any holiday time with your spouse when you had too much closeness? Vacation is often a time with long, hot car rides where personal space is virtually lacking. Janice and Ed will never forget one such trip. We were coming up the I-5 Highway from California in our car without air conditioning. The temperature was at least 100 degrees Fahrenheit. Both of our brains were fried. Ed was wearing sandals while driving because it was so hot. Suffering from a headache, Ed got out of the car at a rest stop and said, "You stepped on my black shoes. What did you do to my shoes?" Janice, who was sitting in the backseat, said, "I did not step on your shoes. I wasn't even sitting there. I didn't touch your shoes at all." After getting out of the car, Ed soaked his hat with water and read a book under a shelter. Janice got into the driver's seat and started slowly driving away. The boys were saying, "Mommy, what are you doing? What about Daddy?" She said, "It's all right. I am just going to drive a little bit, and then I'll come back." A few minutes later Janice came back, and Ed got into the backseat. They didn't talk for about four hours until they got into Oregon, where there was a nice motel in the cool woods. There was a swimming pool where they could cool down, and then they were fine. This incident gave them fresh empathy for inner city riots in the hot summer. Sometimes in our closeness we can get overheated in our relationships.

Conflicted couples, even when distant from each other, are usually focusing mostly on each other.[95] Distancing spouses often take refuge in overwork, substance abuse, or jobs requiring travel. Sometimes one spouse distances from the other by anxiously focusing on their child. Conflicted couples often have the most intense of all relationships.

Bowen described the common syndrome of "too much closeness" as "weekend neurosis" or "cabin fever."[96] Otherwise-nice people will suddenly have a seemingly uncontrollable urge to emotionally cut off from their marital "cabin." They have to get away from each other. Has this ever happened to you? What helps you balance closeness and personal space?

CHAPTER 4

The Dance of Intimacy

The theme of the fourth week of the Strengthening Marriage Workshop was strengthening marriages through balancing closeness and personal space. This balancing can be envisioned as a husband and wife dancing.[97] There is closeness in dancing but there is always space as you go back and forth. Ed and Janice love to dance. Sometimes Ed steps on Janice's toes. Ed's parents met at an Air Force dance, where his dad stepped on his mom's toes. She still let him walk her home. Is dancing part of your marriage? The dance of intimacy at its best is fluid. If you lose your flexibility and become rigid, you lose the life energy of marriage. For the rest of your life, till death do you part, you will be balancing the marital dance of closeness and personal space. What does your dance of intimacy look like these days? Are you willing to learn some new dance steps with your spouse, for better, for worse?

Janice and Ed love holding hands while watching movies together. Hollywood movies often flip back and forth between fused closeness and emotionally cut off distance. The relationship fusion in many movies is vividly expressed in the paradoxical claim, "I can't live with you—I can't live without you." In the Strengthening Marriage Workshop, we gave a Hollywood marital illustration of fusion and resulting emotional cutoff:

> Think of Rhett Butler and Scarlett O'Hara in the classic movie *Gone with the Wind*. What was that relationship like? [comments by participants: fiery, stormy, dramatic]. Then Scarlett was also attracted to Ashley Wilkes. What was he like? [comment: He was a milquetoast.] He probably didn't have much of a sense of self. He eventually married Melanie.[98]

Scarlett O'Hara's relational fusion with Ashley Wilkes and then with Rhett Butler ended both times in painful emotional cutoff. During our Strengthening Marriage Workshop, we had several workshop couples act out this closeness/personal space tension by choosing several different places to stand in the clubhouse while describing their marital interactions. What might your marriage or relationship look like if you similarly acted out your closeness/personal space dynamic?

To reduce emotional cutoff in a married couple, balance is essential, as too little or too much distance creates anxiety. Any lack of balance in a marriage can create a sense of threat.[99] Unless the distance is right, married couples cannot hear each other. The right amount of emotional space increases accurate hearing in a marriage.[100] How much emotional space do you or your spouse need? In the fourth week of the workshop, we commented on the paradox of togetherness:

> The problem with many marital therapies is that these therapies are so focused on togetherness that it is out of balance. Togetherness, closeness, intimacy—we have to do everything together; we have to share everything. But no one can actually live there. You will lose yourself. If togetherness is all that you have, you will actually run from it. You will shut down, or your spouse will shut down. Togetherness is often the problem, not the answer. If you deal with separateness, learning to be your own person, you will get togetherness thrown in.[101]

Surprisingly, the wrong kind of togetherness leads to greater marital anxiety.[102] Bowen named this the "togetherness force." Togetherness and anxiety feed off each other. Kerr and Bowen stated that

> the universal problem for all partnership, marital or otherwise, was not getting closer; it was preserving self in a close relationship, something that no one made of flesh and blood seems to do well. (I eventually came to define my marriage counseling as trying to help people separate so that they would not have to "separate.")[103]

Togetherness has sometimes been painful for us. Ed's a morning person, and Janice is not. He does let Janice sleep in later, sometimes. Janice discovered on our honeymoon that Ed is a very early riser, like his father. He thought Janice should get up at the crack of dawn like he did. Ed insensitively did not realize that Janice loves to sleep in.

Janice was too kind to initially tell him that her time clock was different. Some of Ed's favorite childhood memories were listening to his father's amazing family stories at 6am as they ate their cereal. While on family vacation at Okanagan lake, Ed loved to wake up early and join his father, as they jumped into the cold water while screaming loudly. Then they would go back to the motel room where his mom was still sleeping, and enjoy a hot breakfast. When Ed wakes up early, he is full of energy, and often at his most creative peak, brimming with unexpected new ideas for books and sermons. Much of his doctoral thesis was written in the very early morning. He has had to learn, out of love for Janice, to try to be quiet as a church mouse at 5 am. We even had to get a handyman to remove the early morning squeaks from our bedroom floor. Janice is a much happier wife when she is not sleep-deprived.

Steinke says, "We need to be separate (to be alone, to stand on our own two feet) and to be close (to be together, to stand hand-in-hand)."[104] This is the tension between separateness and closeness. We all need separateness. If you don't find a way to be separate, you will lose self. You will become anxious and actually lose the ability to think clearly. You may end up running from your marriage relationship.

An imbalance of marital closeness and personal space produces either cutoff or fusion. Both cutoff and fusion are at the extreme ends of the closeness–personal space continuum. While fusion is separation anxiety, cutoff is closeness anxiety.[105] They are both pulling in opposite directions. Imagine how marital cutoff uses its emotional booster rocket to leave the earth's atmosphere while fusion tries to keep us on planet earth.

It can be hard to be your own person. Sometimes one's family of origin doesn't make any room for that. But the breakthrough is found in working on being your own person. Your spouse wants to be married to someone who is their own person. When your spouse is anxious, however, they may give you confused signals that make you feel that they want you to be just like them. When you become entangled, you're fused, you're swallowed, you lose identity, and you don't know who you are.

Since Janice has retired, we see each other a lot more and are more in each other's space. Each of us needs closeness. That is why you became married or are considering marriage. We need closeness on the one hand and distance, or separateness, on the other. What does too much distance look like? Sometimes Janice comes in feeling tired. Couples are most vulnerable to conflict when they are experiencing any or all four elements of what the twelve-step movement calls HALT (Hungry, Angry, Lonely, Tired). When Janice is feeling weary, she really doesn't want an intense conversation with Ed. At times, he can be rather intense. She just wants to relax, decompress, and read a book. Janice needs down time. In the past, Ed, being overly fused, might have felt rejected and pursued Janice. Ed also needs his down time, especially after dealing with a long, stressful day. Being a son of an electrical engineer, he finds it relaxing to interact with his 20,000+ social media followers through posting an update on his blog.[106] In the past, Janice, being overly fused to Ed, might have resented that Ed was feeling tired and may have pursued/nagged him. In Janice's Methodist-background family, resting and not working is almost equivalent to sinning. In your family, is it okay to rest? Is it okay to take a break when you are feeling exhausted? What do you and your spouse find most restful and refreshing?

Without emotional closeness, marriages are left with a marked emotional distance, which Bowen called emotional divorce.[107] In thirty-seven years of ordained ministry, we have known many couples who are still under the same roof but are emotionally divorced. We wrote this book because we believe that life can be better than this marital stalemate. The dreams that took you to the altar can be re-captured and reshaped for a new adventure, a new dance. From our forty years of marriage, we can guarantee you that God always has a new adventure just around the corner, if we will just have the eyes to see it and the courage to grasp it. We all want security—we want safety—but it often steals joy, kills adventure, and actually hampers intimacy. Are you willing to choose adventure over security, for better, for worse?

After twenty-three years with Vancouver Coastal Health, Janice began sensing that it was time for her to retire and to downsize our four-bedroom townhouse to a two-bedroom apartment. Ed was initially somewhat resistant. All three of our adult sons, however, had moved out, and we were finished with having any more student homestays. Through extensive prayer and discussion, we began to move forward in this new adventure, for better, for worse. Because we were in agreement, our varying strengths were mobilized in this daunting enterprise. There is remarkable power in marital agreement, in getting on the same page.[108] Listening carefully to our real estate agent, Shane Gray, we radically decluttered our townhouse by 50 percent, even temporarily moving much of our furniture to a storage facility. The townhouse itself underwent numerous minor renovations with the help of a gifted, good friend. To facilitate eight days of viewing by potential buyers, we stayed with relatives and at the Holiday Inn.

On the eighth day, we moved back home, and within five minutes of the deadline we received four offers to buy our townhouse, all above asking price. What a roller coaster adventure. As we made offers for apartments nearer to our family, we had many disappointments. One day, Janice saw a listing that she intuitively knew would be the right place to move. With the help of another gifted real estate agent, Catherine Wolf, the doors opened up. At times, we were both in significant physical pain from the endless "gymnastics" involved in moving house. When we finally moved into our apartment, we were in total chaos, unable to find anything. Marital adventures often include a lot of creative chaos. Looking back, we are grateful that we mutually embraced this adventure of moving. It was the right time, the right place, and the right adventure. Where might you need to declutter in your marriage to get things moving? The gain is worth the pain.

The dance of intimacy can easily degenerate into blaming one's spouse for stepping on one's toes. When couples are convinced that an issue must be immediately resolved, conflict increases. Winning the marital battle becomes everything. Criticism, contempt, and negativity become the dominant note of a former loving relationship. It is very easy to slip into self-righteousness. Ed and Janice both like to be right, but we have discovered over the past forty years that winning the argument never really satisfies. The first step in becoming healthy is when one spouse starts taking responsibility for self and stops blaming their partner.[109] It is sometimes so tempting to blame the ones we love. In the marriage workshop, we challenged the couples to fast for a week from blaming each other. We said to the couples, "Don't try to do this perfectly. But what if you actually reduced the blaming behaviour?" Pointing the finger at our spouse steals energy that we need to use to work on our own issues. How often do you and your spouse step on each other's toes?

Richardson said that "blaming our parents for our problems and unhappiness means we will be prone to blaming whomever else we hook up with in our adult life for our continuing unhappiness."[110] We may tend to blame our parents. So as adults, we will think that we should blame our spouse. Imagine if we could give up blaming. What if we didn't blame ourselves either? Bowen advocated stepping back and getting beyond anger and blame.[111] Dr. E. Stanley Jones once said, "If you are unhappy at home, you should try to find out if your wife hasn't married a grouch." It is remarkable how easily the self-centred part of our brain justifies our angry blaming of our spouse. It can feel so natural, even the right thing to do. Self-pity can be tempting, after all that we have done for our ungrateful spouse. As Richardson put it,

> When we begin to feel anxious, one of the first questions we usually ask is whose fault it is.... Most people decide that the fault lies with the other person when significant, anxiety-stirring difference is discovered.[112]

As a spouse emotionally cuts off, they leave the dance floor either openly or secretly. The non-present spouse may simultaneously pretend, through their pseudo-self, to be present. Sometimes covert marital cutoff is hidden behind a cozy togetherness that masks an internal cutoff. Richardson said marital cutoff "can be as subtle as tuning out of a conversation and turning on the TV or as dramatic as leaving the house, the city, or the country. Many people can live in the same house and still be thousands of miles away emotionally."[113] We may say the right things with our lips, but our hearts may be far away both from our spouse and our God.[114] Where is your heart these days?

The pseudo-self in marriage is an actor wearing a mask.[115] For this reason, the pseudo-self can be very persuasive in acting as if it is engaged and maritally connected. That is why husbands have told me that they didn't know that there were any marital problems until the moving truck arrived. Both those cutting off and those being cut off feel powerless, thinking that the other spouse has the power. Their cutting-off is often a reaction to their own perceived power-lessness.[116] Jack and Judith Balswick commented that when spouses insist on their own way, marriage becomes a dreadful place of vying for power.[117] We should never underestimate our capacity to embrace the darkness of revenge with those whom we have loved and are still fused.

Our people-pleasing and conflict avoidance can drive us to cutoff places that we never intended to go. A good example of marital cutoff would be Romeo and Juliet's marriage. While their Shakespearean marriage was very romantic, it was also immature and short-lived, with their very lives being cut off. We never learned how they might have coped with the challenge of sleep deprivation while changing diapers at 3 am. How much pretending have you done in your current or past marriages? Did your parents ever pretend that everything was all right when it clearly was not? Both pretending and exposing our pretending is a significant theme with Bowen:

> It is easy for most people to detect gross examples of pretense, but there is enough of the imposter in all of us so that it is difficult to detect lesser degrees of the imposter in others.... I consider rugged individualism to be an exaggerated pretend posture of a person struggling against emotional fusion."[118]

The cutoff thinking that accompanies pretending is rigid, narrow, and polarized, with differences and personal issues being avoided. The biblical term for rigidity is stiff-neckedness. Deuteronomy 10:16 encourages us to circumcise our hearts and no longer be stiff-necked. God challenged Ed in 1984 and 1990 at renewal conferences about his hard-heartedness and stiff neck.[119] The flip side of Ed's Scottish-heritage strength of perseverance is his stubbornness and rigidity. Jesus was at times angered and deeply distressed by people's stubborn hearts.[120] In Acts 7:51, Stephen said to his listeners, "You are stiff-necked and uncircumcised in heart. Just like your ancestors, you always resist the Holy Spirit." Because people don't like to be told that they and their parents are rigid, they stoned Stephen to death. How rigid was your parents' marriage? How rigid is your current marriage? Do you ever resist the still, small voice of the Holy Spirit in your marriage?

CHAPTER 5

When You're Understood, You Can Put Up with Almost Anything

*Inside the heart of each and every one of us, there is a
longing to be understood by someone who really cares. When
a person is understood, he or she can put up with almost
anything in the world.*

E d penned those words in 1991 in his column for a local newspaper in North Vancouver. He had no idea how far outside his local sphere of influence these words would travel. When he did a recent Google search, he discovered nearly 19,000 links to his column! He was amazed to find that those words have been posted on thousands of strangers' blogs, social networking pages, and romance-oriented websites.

Romance is all about "inside the heart of every one of us." Women buy tens of millions of romance novels each year because they are longing for a heart-felt connection. One of our deepest needs is to be truly understood. Women are often longing for a man who understands them. Some mistakenly think this is impossible. They're convinced that their concerns and problems are so unique that they'll be misunderstood outsiders forever. Many hope that if they get married, their partner will automatically understand them. When that doesn't happen, they become even more frustrated. Why do we so often misunderstand our spouse? Both Jesus and Paul connect our lack of understanding to hardness of heart.[121] Dr. Cecil Osborne, counsellor and author of *The Art of Understanding Your Mate*, once said, "Marriage is the most rewarding and the most difficult relationship known to man."[122]

How romantic are you? Do you long for more romance in your

marriage? Alfred Lord Tennyson wrote, "If I had a flower for every time I thought of you, I could walk in my garden forever."[123] If you haven't been romancing your spouse lately, they may be suspicious of your initial efforts, and it may feel as if you're romancing a stony heart. This is where perseverance and gentleness are so vital in the pursuit. For example, Janice needs to know that, as far as Ed's concerned, she's the most beautiful woman on earth, a precious gift from God to him. But she also finds it very romantic when Ed takes out the garbage or does the dishes! Ed finds it romantic when Janice takes time to edit his articles and listens to him when he wants to bounce around a new idea for a book. Romance is saying, as Robert Browning did, "Grow old along with me! The best is yet to be."[124] Do you yearn for "till death do us part" romance? Bridging emotional cutoff is very romantic.

CHAPTER 6

Bridging Emotional Cutoff

E motional Cutoff primarily describes how people disconnect from their past in order to begin their lives in the current generation.[125] When the dance of intimacy leads to emotional cutoff, what then? Gilbert compassionately asked the following questions about emotional cutoff:

> Is there anything I might do to bridge the cutoff? Is there a way I can work to lower my emotional intensity so that cutoff will not be inevitable in the future?[126]

It is encouraging to know that marital cutoff is not an emotional death sentence that we are fatalistically doomed to endure. Ferrera stated,

> Cutoffs can be bridged and reversed; contact can be reestablished; and people can reclaim to a significant extent the emotional connection and stability that has been lost through cutoff.[127]

As Christ-followers, this is good news. Romance can be rediscovered. Through learning about emotional cutoff, blind spots can be removed. Neutrality and curiosity reduces cutoff. Being emotionally cut off can go either way: either making couples more defensive toward each other or more desperate for a better way. Bridging cutoff requires recognition of the existing marital fusion.[128] It is often difficult to recognize emotional fusion because it feels so normal. It may be all that we know generationally. A first step in bridging cutoff might be to name our blindness about how fused we probably are.

In 2014, shortly after finishing his doctorate, Ed went blind in his right eye. This blindness was not noticeable until Ed was at the University of British Columbia trying to read tiny 19th century print.

Upon going to an eye specialist, Ed discovered that he did not have cataracts, glaucoma, retinal detachment, or macular degeneration. Over time, the gel, or vitreous, in our eyes shrinks and detaches from the retina. In rare cases, as with Ed, it sticks and causes a microscopic macular hole. Before 1970, they could not do anything about this. After laser surgery, Dr. Kirker filled Ed's right eye with gas, which temporarily held everything in place. In order for the gas to do its job, he had to be horizontal for 90% of the time. Fortunately, he was able to rent a massage desk and full-body massage pillow. Janice was very kind and supportive to Ed during this ordeal, even getting him *talking books* from the local library. Lying face down for three days was a brand new experience for him. It gave Ed a new understanding of the line from Hank Williams' hit song *I Saw The Light:* "Then like the blind man that God gave back his sight." Similarly, Family Systems Theory gives us new eyes to see our marriage dynamics where we were previously blind. Where might you be blind in your relationship? Your new eyes are key to bridging emotional cutoff in your family.

When we first attempt to bridge multigenerational cutoff, some may see us as betraying our family equilibrium and going over to the enemy. Richardson said, "The main reason we usually [hesitate] to bridge the major cutoffs in our families is because we believe that some other member of the family that we are close to will be upset."[129] Imagine how horrendously difficult it would have been to attempt to bridge the physical and emotional cutoff that occurred between post–World War II German neighbours who were Jewish and Gentile. I am reminded here of how difficult it was for Corrie Ten Boom, who told the story of her concentration camp experience in her book *The Hiding Place,* to choose to shake the hand of her repentant German concentration camp guard.[130] Naively attempting to bridge cutoff without a clear understanding can be like throwing a match on gasoline.[131]

Reducing emotional cutoff requires that marital closeness needs to be a choice. There is often pressure and obligation when people think, "We're married. We have to be close." One of the times married couples fight the most is around Valentine's Day, because there is pressure that February 14 has to be a romantic evening. One year, Ed had not bothered to make a reservation for Valentine's Day. Janice was upset about this, so she decided that they should go to a little restaurant that they had seen on Lonsdale Avenue. Unfortunately, the place was not clean, and the food was terrible. It was not a very romantic Valentine's Day. They never went back.

Pressurized obligation doesn't work. Does your spouse ever pressure you? Do you ever pressure them? Steinke said that "genuine closeness is always chosen; it is not driven, forced or obligated togetherness."[132] Two people swallowing one another is not a relationship. That's emotional fusion. What if we dropped the obligation? What if we stopped comparing ourselves to other people's marriages and actually worked on our own marriage? What if we stopped trying to be somebody else? As our marriages become more goal oriented and future focused, bridging cutoff becomes more possible.

Bridging marital cutoff changes the brain and physiology of the individual.[133] This is a long process that needs to be worked on throughout one's marriage.[134] Bowen said that there are people who never separate from their parents and—all things being equal—will remain attached forever.[135] Fused attachment to one's parents hampers healthy connection with one's spouse. As Genesis 2:24 and Matthew 19:5 teach us, marital cleaving is dependent upon parental leaving. To what degree have you emotionally left and self-differentiated from your parents? Marital leaving is not the same as emotionally cutting off from your parents. Part of the marriage dance is to detach without cutting off. Emotional detachment rather than emotional cutoff is the healthy way forward. To detach is to be freed from unbalanced attachment to your parents."[136] Our unresolved attachments are usually parental, but they affect every other relationship.

Janice remembers wanting to move away and get a fresh start after Ed graduated with his master's. But Ed wanted to stay near family, and his mother did not want him to leave. Out of the blue, Ed was offered a position in Vancouver that he had not applied for. In taking this "plum" position, Ed had no idea how complicated it would be and how much unresolved conflict there was at that church. For better or worse, it was while serving at that church that Ed lost his voice for eighteen months before having throat surgery.

The greater the unresolved attachment, the less one can be a self with one's spouse and with one's parents. No one becomes an adult without some unresolved emotional attachment.[137] We are all a work in progress. Bowen said,

> One of the most important functional patterns in a family has to do with the intensity of the unresolved emotional attachment to parents, most frequently to the mother for both men and women, and the way the individual handles the attachment. All people have an emotional attachment to their parents that is more intense than most people permit themselves to believe.[138]

It is very easy to stay stuck in denial about attachment issues. Few of us are objective about our parents.[139] The more we deny our unresolved emotional attachment, the greater the power of emotional cutoff in our marriages. How intense is your attachment to your parents? Have you ever known someone who spends all their extra time with either their father or mother rather than with their spouse? We have seen this. One of our pastor friends told the story of his very controlling mother who treated his new wife badly. The mother never wanted to spend time with his wife. Finally, this man differentiated by saying to his mother that if she didn't change and treat his wife kindly, his mother would not be invited to their house any more. He realized his wife had to come first. Fortunately, the mother was willing to grow and change.

CHAPTER 7

From Couch to Coach

Pastoral coaching helps reduce marital cutoff. Are you open to the idea of being coached? The Bowen model prefers the term "coaching," shifting from couch to coach.[140] A basic premise of Bowen Theory is that married couples can find their own answers if they work on it. The pastoral coach, like a sports coach, may diagram the patterns or plays and assists in developing a game plan or goal-oriented vision. But it is up to the couple to implement the game plan.[141]

The pastoral coach is a calming presence that reduces the tendency of the married couple to vent, dump on each other, and emotionally cut off. It is easy to regress while bridging marital cutoff without the encouragement of a coach. Ed remembers being reluctant to receive coaching when getting married. Even though he had never been married before, he had read many books on marriage and thought that he had it all figured out. At age 22, Ed naively saw himself as very mature. Little did he know that real-life marriage is more complicated than words on a page. Janice was also reluctant to receive pre-marital coaching, as she was very private and had Ed on a pedestal. He could do no wrong, just like her father. We were given the Taylor/Johnson personality test, which suggested that we were significantly different from each other. This test proved to be very accurate.

Pastoral coaches may find themselves pressured to unwisely accept responsibility for other couples' unsolvable problems. If they accept responsibility for the anxiety of the married couple, they are actually being uncaring and robbing the couple of their opportunity for growth. Objective neutrality by the coach is a gift to the couple. Pastoral coaches are to be ready, in the spirit of 1 Peter 3:15, to give an answer when people ask, doing it with gentleness and respect. Family Systems Theory epitomizes the gentleness and respect that may lead people to ask us about our hope within. Friedman taught that coaches are to promise no benefits except those that come from the couple's own effort to learn about themselves and change themselves.[142] The couple responds best when coaches are clear about what they can or cannot do. By matching people's energy, they encourage the couple to accept responsibility for their own change. Matching someone's energy means working with couples who are motivated to change. It is counterproductive to pressure people into changing or to set marriage goals far beyond their willingness to grow. Any goals must be discerned and embraced by the couple.

CHAPTER 8

Emotional Cutoff and Symptoms

E motional cutoff produces marital symptoms. The older Freudian model tends to see symptoms as indications of intrapsychic
diseases within the patient. The Bowen model instead sees
symptoms as indications of a wider emotional system that transcends
the mere individual.[143] We may be tempted to identify one person in a
marriage or family as the problem, but marriage problems are family
problems, not just the problems of one individual. Family problems
require family solutions.

Observing symptoms is key to strengthening a marriage. Kerr
and Bowen viewed symptoms such as over/under eating, over/under
achieving, excessive alcohol/drug use, and affairs as indicators of
having given up too much self, often absorbing anxiety within the
marital relationship system. Ironically, said Kerr and Bowen, conflicted couples sometimes have fewer symptoms, because their conflict
"can provide a very strong sense of emotional contact" with the other
spouse.[144] Chronic symptoms are sometimes a diversion from the
most challenging relationship problems of the couple and/or family.[145]
Nagging and pursuing by the wife is often a symptom of her loneli-
ness when her husband will not share his ideas and thoughts with her.
His emotional distance from his wife may be a way of reducing his
anxiety over his fusion and loss of self with his wife. Many couples
blame all their marriage problems on a lack of communication. While
this claim makes common sense, it may be misdirected. Gilbert suggested that communication is less a problem than a symptom.[146]

Who is most vulnerable to developing symptoms in marriage? Kerr
and Bowen suggested that the compliant spouse picks up the anxiety
projected from the dominant spouse, becoming more anxiously at
risk for a symptom.[147] Domineering attitudes, such as controlling,
criticism, and blaming, encourage emotional cutoff. We have seen a

number of couples develop symptoms of overeating, alcohol abuse, and sexual escapades when their chronic anxiety became more acute. Often these couples temporarily suppressed the symptoms by over-focusing on the children. This proved to be a short-term "solution," as the symptoms would come back with a vengeance. Few of these couples were willing to do the significant personal work that could have brought a lasting alleviation of these symptoms. What symptoms have you observed in difficult marriages?

CHAPTER 9

Removing the Log from Our Eye

The more we nonjudgmentally observe, the less we cut off in our marriage. Most of us, as Jesus taught, have a log in our eye that blinds us from seeing the obvious.[148] Jesus challenged us to remove the log from our own eye before we try to take the splinter out of another person's eye. Such blindness is rooted in the difficulty of seeing things that do not fit your worldview. We underestimate how difficult it can be to perceive things that we do not want to see. One has to become an observer before it is possible to see.[149] The less we see, the more we disconnect from each other. The more we see, the greater our neutrality. Conversely the greater the neutrality, the more we see in our marriage.

Ed and Janice lacked this neutrality for many years. Janice liked to spend money, buying pretty things and clothes. Ed didn't want to spend money, wanting only to save it. Janice would get upset if Ed tried to slow down her spending. The things were on sale, just for that week. When the bills came in, there would be tension over how to juggle the finances. In more recent years, we have developed more neutrality around our spending and saving habits and are more able to objectively discuss finances without blaming or cutting off.

The ideal neutrality, said Daniel Papero, is like quietly watching the ripples of a mountain pond.[150] Gilbert and Bowen likened such neutral observing to putting on a lab coat like a scientist or watching from a space craft. Bowen compared this to moving from a playing field to the top of a stadium to watch a football game.[151] This observational discipline is like making use of a personal trainer at a gym. Many people turn up at the gym in January, hoping for the post-Christmas quick fix. By February, discouragement and dropout set in for many. It is too easy to lose heart and give up.[152] Learning to become an observational scientist in one's marriage is just as challenging. It takes time to retrain and develop the power of observation. This is, in fact, a lifetime project till death do us part. Through developing our observational biceps, we still have feelings but they don't control us. They don't dominate our life decisions or define our core self. This is not about being a 21st-century unfeeling Dr. Spock of *Star Trek* fame. As Richardson commented,

> Being differentiated does not mean becoming unfeeling. Well-differentiated people never lose touch with their feelings, and they can experience and express feelings when necessary. They recognize feelings as one source of information about what is going on in their lives. They can also be passionate in their feelings if they choose. The critical element in a well-differentiated person is this choice. They can decide whether or not to act on feelings. [153]

It was encouraging to see how many of the Strengthening Marriage Workshop participants embraced this new way of seeing. Thinking like a scientist, which reduces observational blindness, holds great promise for bridging marital cutoff. Reducing emotional cutoff through increasing one's objectivity is very demanding. Objectivity for Bowen was about each person stepping back and thoughtfully looking around, without needing to change one's partner's point of view.[154] Such objectivity, said Bowen, is rarer than people think. Many spouses are merely pretending to be objective.[155] Are we willing to own our part, for better, for worse? Owning our part in times of conflict is very challenging because we are often so remarkably blind and defensive. How willing are you to accept influence from your spouse? As Jeremiah 17:9 painfully reminds us, our hearts are deceitful above all things. Reducing cutoff requires a radically objective assessment of one's self, not just one's spouse. Objectivity is at the heart of the key Family Systems concept of differentiation. The more objective we become, the more we can act to bring lasting change in our marriage.[156] In the Strengthening Marriage Workshop, we taught several times over the four weeks on the concept of objectivity:

> Objectivity means for each of us in our marriage to become almost like a scientist or a space astronaut observing ourselves

and our own marriage. We need that little bit of detachment, but that is hard because we tend to become swallowed in the intensity of our emotions. If we can become objective, it does something remarkable…. What if we didn't blame ourselves either? What if we became an observer, a scientist, someone who is looking for understanding rather than blaming? … What if we said: "I'm going to watch this. I can feel my blaming coming on. I am going to slow down, have a coffee and watch what is happening"? … You have to, at some point, be neutral about the very marriage that you are committed to, not that you cease to be committed but that you have a degree of detachment from your emotions. You begin to watch yourself and your marriage like a scientist.[157]

In coaching a couple, Bowen used to say, "Give me a few minutes of your most objective thinking."[158] So often in marriage conflict, we are swallowed by our subjective, unexamined emotions. Thinking about our thinking regarding our marriage is the Bowenian way forward: What were the patterns of the thoughts, and what kind of working conclusions came from thinking about your relationship? How objective is your thinking about your marriage?

CHAPTER 10

Reducing our Marital Reactivity

How emotionally reactive are you in your marriage? When people become upset, they may reactively yell, blame, or go to silence and cutoff. Reactivity is the opposite of thoughtful responsiveness, in which one retains the power of choice. Emotional reactivity in married couples is associated with rigid inflexibility and demanding the other person to change. How adaptable are you to making room for your spouse in your already busy schedule? When reactivity takes over, we lose a sense of proportion. In our reactivity, we end up trying to control our spouse in order to regain our sense of personal control. How controlling are you at times?

The higher our emotional reactivity, the greater is the likelihood of marital cutoff. Likewise, the higher the marital conflict, the greater is the emotional reactivity. As a spouse increases awareness and control of their own emotional reactivity, cutoff is reduced. The more we understand, the less we react.[159] Would you like to reduce your emotional reactivity, your need to control?

Nichols taught that the single greatest impediment to understanding one another is our tendency to become emotionally reactive.[160] Sometimes a spouse who is not feeling listened to will anxiously chase their spouse until they get a reaction.[161] The rugged individualist's determination to be independent often stems more from his reactivity to other people than from a thoughtfully determined direction for self.

Janice knows of a woman who would reactively nag her husband and chase him around the apartment, trying to get him to talk to her about a problem with their child. The husband didn't say anything and just kept walking away, stonewalling her. Eventually she became so angry that she moved out and stayed with a girlfriend for a few days. We unknowingly had this couple for dinner during this separation. The husband was so upset about her leaving that he actually told us, breaking the silence. The wife's eyes flashed with fire as she said that he wouldn't deal with the problem. We were privileged to coach this couple and pray with them about potential solutions. She went back home, and new boundaries were set with the child.

Behind our stubborn reactivity is the fear of loss of self, that we will be swallowed up and disappear.[162] Such reactive fear causes us to cut off rather than become a non-person. We may reactively see ourselves as victimized by our stubborn, unloving, illogical spouse.[163] We perceive ourselves as having been treated unfairly, and we are not going to give in. Marital cutoff often brings emotional stuckness, denial of issues, frozen anger, and conflict avoidance. As we accept appropriate responsibility for our life, we decrease the cutoff. Being more responsible rather than reactive involves owning our own mistakes, reducing blaming our spouse, and working on controlling our temper. How are you at accepting responsibility for your choices? Are you similar or different to your parents in this area?

Marital reactivity is like an auto-immune dysfunction. Reactivity involves the amygdala, the third section of the brain at the back of your head. That's the source of the fight-or-flight response, when we just react. It's not a thinking response. It's the kind of reaction you might have to a forest fire or a burglar. The cortisol in your brain fires. The part that does the thinking and the choosing, the neocortex, is in the front of your brain. The neocortex is where you want to live out your marriage. Most people live their marriage out of their amygdala. You have to train yourself, which takes time, to switch from this reactivity to a thinking response. You train yourself to be more responsive by focusing on strengths, particularly the strengths of your spouse. That is one of the ways that you shift your brain. The amygdala always focuses on weaknesses, threats, reactivity: "It will all go to hell in a handbasket; the sky's falling; there is no future, and you might as well give up." That's what the amygdala does to us.

By being non-reactive and focusing on marital strengths, we set the emotional thermostat in the room.[164] In the Strengthening Marriage Workshop, we taught couples about the marital immune system, saying,

If you don't have a marital immune system, then what happens to two different bodies that don't have immune systems if they touch? They get infected. They get sick. They sometimes instantly implode. So how can two very different people in a marriage get close without imploding? Focusing on strengths enhances our immune system; it reduces our reactivity. You may experience a primal response when your spouse upsets you, pushes your buttons, and triggers you. Reactivity, according to Richardson, is our anxious response to a perceived threat. When you are feeling attacked, what do you do? You can get defensive. You may want to verbally attack back. This is not a thinking response; it is a gut-level response. It is basically an anxiety response. So, by focusing on your strengths, it actually reduces your tendency to be reactive.

What limits us in helping other married couples? Perhaps it is the vicious cycle of our personal emotional reactivity, which limits our ability to think clearly and be non-reactive with other couples. In order to best help other married couples, we need to become more aware of our own personal reactivity, defensiveness, and tendency to cut off. The heart is the heart of the matter, especially in marriage. King David prayed, "Search me, God, and know my heart."[165] People look at the outward appearance, but God looks at the heart.[166] The Bible mentions the heart 750 times. It is the very core of who we really are without any pretending. Self-examination of the heart is an ancient Judeo-Christian discipline that can bear much fruit in our marriage.[167] What might it be like if we turned our heart back again to our spouse and even to our God?

Have you ever sung the song "Change My Heart, O God," and really meant it?[168] What might be holding you back from radical heart change in your marriage? It can be very difficult to see our own defensiveness. Ed will never forget when lay pastor Jeannie Lynn, at St Matthew's Abbotsford, shared something important with him. He thanked Jeannie and asked her why she hadn't shared it before. Jeannie simply said, "You wouldn't have listened." How much are we missing in our marriage because of our defensive reactivity?

CHAPTER 11

Asking the Right Marital Questions

What if we told you that your marriage can be radically transformed through thoughtful questions? Titelman said that Bowen was anti-technique in his coaching style.[169] The use of process questions is as close as Bowen came to a technique. Process questions with married couples include who, what, where, when, and how. The benefits of process questions are that they help explore the space between you as a couple, slow down and diminish reactivity, and encourage self-reflective thoughtfulness.[170] Bowen Theory carefully avoids our automatic preoccupation with why something may have happened in our marriage. Family Systems thinking focuses on what we do and not on our verbal explanations about why we do it. The use of "why" questions cause us to lose our focus on the couple relationship. "Why" questions in marriage are often avoidance behaviour.[171] It is not easy to give up asking about the motivation, the why question. Why, you might ask, is it so hard to stop asking why? Asking why seems to be a residual, regressive reaction when we are traumatized and grieved. "Why" sometimes screams within us, yet answers rarely satisfy the ache. In the Strengthening Marriage Workshop, we taught over several weeks on the priority of process questions:

> The questions you want to ask are not "why" questions, such as "Mom, why did you do this? Dad, why didn't you do that?" You need to ask who, what, where, when, and how questions.... Family Systems Theory is about asking good questions. You could write in your journal, "I am feeling tempted to blame right now. What is happening?" Drop the whys, which just makes you angrier. "Why" is often an angry question: "Why's that?" What if you reduced your "whys" this week and went for the when, what, who, how, and where?

Would you be willing to journal about this during the upcoming week?

Friedman described this use of questions as being a catalyst, enabling the couple to "bounce off" the coach to each other.[172] Insightful questions help protect coaches from being overfunctioning rescuers. To overfunction is to do too much in a way that brings emotional fusion with others, loss of self, and a reduction of others' functioning. Bailing others out does not strengthen marriages. We are not called to save or change another person's marriage. Thoughtful questions leave the couple in their own quandary, thereby allowing them to potentially own their own process. Friedman observed that 80 percent of his Family Systems Theory coaching was asking questions.[173] Questions are intended to be low-key and calm. Rather than being advice-giving, process questions help the married couple to more objectively see their role in the emotional system.[174]

One couple that Janice and Ed coached had a tendency to blame each other when stressed. We had them look at their family background, which enabled them to see that this was a generational pattern. We asked them thoughtful questions about their marriage and family, which began to give them some more objectivity and curiosity about each other. It has been remarkable to see the reduction in blaming. Instead this couple have learned to affirm each other's differences.

Bowen used nonconfrontational questions to avoid taking marital sides. His goal was to stimulate thinking more than to encourage expression of feelings. When feelings or tears emerged, Bowen would calmly ask, "What was the thought that stimulated the tears?" or ask the other what they were thinking when the feeling started.[175] What do you think of these process questions? Would you like to try one with your spouse? Here is a sample question to get you started: What has it been like for you to read this book?

CHAPTER 12

The Avoider Can Always Outrun the Pursuer

Pursuing your spouse doesn't work. They can always outrun you.[176] Steinke says that pursuit behaviour is any behaviour that overfocuses on another person. The most obvious form of such behaviour is rescue.[177] Is it good to focus on your spouse or your children? Yes. But overfocus will take them out. Do you overfocus and pursue in your marriage? What if you chose to make yourself small instead? What if you did a little experiment and had your spouse practise pursuing you instead? That might be a stretch, but you could try it. Pursuing is also closely connected to overfunctioning. The overfunctioning pursuer can choose to dial down and reduce their overfunctioning. When Ed used to chase Janice, she would hide. Then Ed would pursue her more, and Janice would still hide and get angrier with Ed. Then after Ed became upset and went away, Janice would pursue him. Ed discovered that at different times he has been an avoider and a pursuer. This insight has been fundamental to gradually shifting his way of relating to Janice.

Ed was shocked during his doctoral studies when he realized the uselessness of his pursuing. So he asked his doctoral adviser, Paddy Ducklow, "If pursuing, rescuing, and fixing people doesn't work, what can you do?" Ducklow said, "K.I.T." (which stands for keep in touch).[178] When your spouse has been running from you and avoiding you, does it work trying to reason with them? You have to wait until they stop running from you. Sometimes, if you will just keep in touch in a gentle, non-reactive way, then the moment may come when they may actually move toward you. You can see that with wounded cats and dogs. If you chase them, they will attack you or run from you. But if you keep in touch, quite often they will come to you. Your spouse can only hear you when they are moving toward you. You may have heard the story of the prodigal son who ran away from his dad, and finally came to himself, returning home. His dad, who had patiently waited for a long time, welcomed his son with open arms.[179] Your spouse is worth the wait. Are your arms currently open or closed to your spouse?

An overfunctioner is someone who wants to control every aspect of the marriage and sometimes boss the other spouse around. Underfunctioners want to get along, and will let themselves be bossed around even if they don't like it. Both overfunctioning and underfunctioning increase the likelihood of emotional cutoff in marriage. Therapists sometimes joke that every overfunctioner deserves their underfunctioner. With married couples, one is often an overfunctioner and the other a dependent underfunctioner. Sometimes in the same marriage, people flip back and forth between overfunctioning and underfunctioning, depending on the issue at hand.

Overfunctioners often, not always, marry underfunctioners. Sometimes there are two overfunctioners or two underfunctioners in a marriage. Overfunctioners tend to take over the other person's space. The other person will underfunction more. Rescuers can't tolerate healthy distance between themselves and others. Have any of you ever had any tendency to be a rescuer? Rescuing takes us out and takes out other people. It can cause our spouse to underfunction or to run. Rescuing is a dead end.

Overfunctioning is about doing too much to gratify one's need to be somebody. Such "do-er" people have a magnetic appeal to underfunctioners. Overfunctioning may cause "dis-integration" in the underfunctioners.[180] The over/underfunctioning dynamic can even flare up unexpectedly into marital violence.[181] Our goal is to turn you as a married couple into systems specialists, ready for when future anxiety inevitably hits your emotional system.[182]

Ed discovered while doing his doctorate that he, like many clergy, was an overfunctioner. When he experimented with reducing his overfunctioning, it shocked some people. Overfunctioners must either willingly let go of overresponsibility or its very weight will force them to do so. Kerr and Bowen contend that

> An overfunctioning person may get sick by virtue of being required by others and requiring of himself more than he can

realistically accomplish…. In time, the overfunctioning one can "absorb" a disproportionate amount of the family problem. As the process progresses, she [or he] feels increasingly overloaded, overwhelmed, and unsupported.[183]

Nothing fuses married couples like one spouse overfunctioning in the other's space.[184] Fusion is the counterfeit of genuine marital intimacy, because it robs the spouse of their personhood. Bowen holds that "recovery can begin with the slightest decrease of the overfunctioning." It is much easier to get the overfunctioner to reduce their overfunctioning than the other way around.[185] Reducing our marital overfunctioning can include more self-effacing humour, more balance in being and doing, more peaceful presence, more honesty, more developing of character and virtue, more safe silences, more playful adventure, more creative dating, and less pressuring each other to conform to one's expectations.[186] How might you like to experiment with reducing overfunctioning in your marriage?

A playful adventure that helped reduce overfunctioning was when Janice went with Ed for her first time to Hawaii. We creatively dated through going on a submarine (where we literally turned blue), visiting survivors at Pearl Harbour, and attending an authentic luau with fire stick dancers. A less pleasant part of the Hawaiian adventure was Ed getting food poisoning and ending up in emergency just before our flight home. The suspense increased when Ed discovered that our extended medical coverage was malfunctioning overseas because of a Canadian computer glitch. This motivated Ed to get well very quickly so that we could take the overnight flight back to Vancouver. Marital adventures have their unexpected challenges.

When your spouse has been running from you and avoiding you, does it work to try to reason with them? You have to wait until they stop running from you. It is the overfunctioner who can bring breakthrough by making themselves small. Instead of rescuing and overfunctioning, what they learn to do is match their spouse's energy level rather than pursuing and chasing.

Who theoretically wants more closeness, the pursuer or the avoider? It appears to be the pursuer, but it's not actually. It looks as though the pursuer wants more closeness, but often pursuers use the pursuit as a way of driving away the avoider, as a means of preserving distance and personal space. They look as if they are the "good person" who is wanting relationship. Pursuers are often the one who will initially contact the marriage counsellor. They will say, "My spouse doesn't want relationship." They will try to get the counsellor to pursue their spouse. Do you think that will work? Not at all. Richardson recommends that a key to breakthrough is for the coach not to pursue the avoider but rather to pursue the pursuer.[187] Then the avoider will quite often come into the relationship.

CHAPTER 13

Valuing Marital Anxiety

How you observe and manage anxiety is key to strengthening your marriage and reducing cutoff. There is a chronic anxiety in all of life that comes with the territory of living. The greater the level of anxiety, the more that our marital behaviour becomes automatic or instinctual. Anxious spouses are often painful to be around, sometimes leading to emotional cutoff.[188] We need to get over our fear of anxiety. As we become less anxious about being anxious, we become freer in our marriages. Bowen reminded us:

> Anxiety does not harm people. It only makes them feel uncomfortable. It can cause you to shake, or lose sleep, or become confused, or develop physical symptoms, but it will not kill you and it will subside. People can even grow and become more mature by having to face and deal with anxiety situations.[189]

Chronic anxiety is sometimes called emotional pain. It is almost like being burned by fire. Of all the relationship patterns, people caught in conflict are most apt to seek help because of their awareness of pain. Growth comes from increasing the pain threshold, not reducing the pain.[190] That is why Friedman memorably commented, "I am on the side of pain."[191] The benefits of marital pain, like those of ingrown toenails, are often underrated. Both can get us to the doctor. What is your relationship pain level these days?

Most people who have come to us for coaching are in significant pain. They don't know how to improve the relationship with their spouse or significant other. Outwardly they may look very successful, but inwardly there may be a quiet desperation. Many are not feeling loved and cared for. Often their spiritual connecting with Christ prompts them to hope against hope that things might change in their marriage. Sometimes the anxiety around their marriage starts to destabilize other functional areas of their lives, including their work and children.

The most contagious of all emotions is anxiety, followed by depression. Anxiety rubs off on people, being transmitted and absorbed without thinking.[192] A married couple doesn't have to choose someone else's anxiety, any more than one chooses someone else's flu or cold. All that has to happen is for the other spouse to "sneeze" anxiously on the partner while their emotional immune system is low. Have you ever "picked up" someone's anxiety? You can receive a phone call, an email, a Facebook post, a Skype call or anything. Before you know it, suddenly you have these feelings in your gut. It's in the back of your neck. It may affect your sleep. It's very painful, like it's stuck inside of you.

Anxiety can seriously reduce our ability to think. We may lack the clarity that we usually count on to make good decisions. It can also reduce the ability of couples to see the big picture, the emotional system. Anxiety can dehumanize the key people in our generational family.[193] Running away from anxiety is impossible, because it is chained like a ball or a pet rock to our ankle. It always comes along for the ride. The anxiety of life, as with Jonah's whale, has a way of chasing us until we stop running from who we are and are called to be.

Janice remembers feeling anxious when she had to play at a recital without her music. She would become so nervous that her hands would shake and she would not be able to remember the music. Janice learned that she had to have her music with her in order to manage her anxiety. Through prayer and counselling, Janice is now much less anxious and more able to enjoy the gift of music.

Anxiety comes down through the generations. One cannot cut one's self off from multigenerational anxiety but only from the knowledge of the sources of marital anxiety. Such cutoff causes anxious spouses to "fly blind" relationally, without any generational, emotional map. Cutoff causes us to minimize our past and exaggerate our present. Despite Hollywood notions, our current spouses were never meant to be our everything. Putting the full weight on the present moment is like driving a three-tonne tractor onto a frozen Canadian pond that was intended only for one small boy practising hockey. We need the older generations to help our present marriages bear the weight of life's inevitable anxieties.

When the cerebral cortex is flooded with anxiety, this creates groupthink, an anxious, fused imitation of actual thinking. Groupthink simulates thinking, using the appearance of reason to whitewash anxiety.[194] Ninety percent of our so-called thoughts, on average, are actually the same thoughts that we had the day before. Repetitive thinking is pretend thinking. Appearances can be deceiving. Reasonable thinking is less common than many realize. A lot of substance abuse is a way of shutting down the pain of thoughtful thinking. Have you ever heard others say "Don't go there. I don't want to think about it."? Anxiety also can shut down our curiosity and willingness to learn more about our marriage. The loss of curious learning increases emotional cutoff. [195] Marital learning takes courage to stay thoughtfully engaged rather than anxiously disconnect.

The restoration of curiosity and imagination brings greater intimacy, both physically and emotionally. A common problem with marriages is that we often think that we have each other figured out: "I know what you are going to say. I know where this is going." Familiarity breeds emotional blindness. As we become a systems thinker, we see differently, and our marital curiosity and imagination increases. That is the goal. If you want a better marriage, increase your imagination, increase your curiosity. What if we dropped the anxious blaming and increased the curiosity for better, for worse? What if we dropped all the judgments and said, "Oh, I wonder what that is all about"?

Children are naturally curious. We need to be child-like, not childish. Many marriages are childish without much childlikeness. Curiosity is at the heart of being child-like. Nagging, screaming, and yelling are signs of being anxiously childish. Enlarging our capacity for imagination and curiosity frees us from the prison of marital anxiety. What if we dreamed outside of the box instead of being rigid in our marriages? We need to be willing to stretch ourselves, to dream, and to seek to understand our spouse, for better, for worse. Sadly, as we become older, often our worlds can shrink. We can become unnecessarily old in our brains. Ed and Janice want to keep growing in curiosity and never grow old, in that sense. Where might you grow in curiosity about your marriage relationship? What intrigues you most about your spouse?

With reduced anxiety, family members become more objective and calmer.[196] Gilbert recommended going to the gym as a way of reducing marital anxiety, something that Ed has been doing for over twenty years, thanks to his wife leading the way. It is not only the marriage that prays together but also the marriage that plays together that stays together. When anxiety is less, many of our marital problems simply don't happen.[197] Less anxiety means less potential emotional cutoff in our marriages. The more self-aware we are, the more observant we become regarding what escalates anxiety. Have you noticed that it sometimes comes in waves, occasionally feeling like a tsunami? Bowen Theory encourages us to pay particular attention to the intensity and duration of anxiety.

In our relationally cut off and fragmented society, we tend to see togetherness as the cure-all for most of our problems. Weddings and togetherness are not a quick fix for our own personal issues. There is no automatic happily-ever-after card.[198] Marriage in no way guarantees emotional maturity. It is a mark of maturity to know what pleases our spouse and to make the special effort to do what pleases them. Immaturity with high anxiety is a difficult combination for couples.[199] Immature people, when anxious, tend to become upset and don't know how to calm down. Bowen said that immaturity causes us to confuse ourselves with God, as if we were omniscient and omnipotent regarding our spouse.[200] Spouses make a very poor substitute for God.

Our post-modern culture simultaneously marginalizes marriages and raises marital expectations.[201] When a couple has unrealistic expectations of themselves, it fosters unhealthy conflict. These can include the expectation that one spouse has to preserve the peace and harmony, or that one spouse knows what is best for the other spouse. People nowadays are sometimes pressuring their own spouse to over-function in superhuman, godlike ways.[202] This can lead to an "anxious hovering," which impairs the other spouse's ability to function. In what way might you lower your expectations of your spouse? How might that reduce the anxiety level in your marriage?

The avoidance of anxiety explains why many married couples are connected by a "rubber band," where they pull away during high anxiety only to snap back into fused togetherness.[203] Richardson says that "to be fused is to be stuck in the tar of a symbiotic or parasitic relationship."[204] So, when you are fused, you are actually feeding off each other like emotional parasites. It doesn't sound like a very healthy image of marriage, does it? Are you currently stuck in the tar? All of us to some degree are emotionally fused. How would you like to get unstuck from any tar in your relationship so that you can actually be yourself? It's far more interesting to be yourself. Gossip and marital anxiety are very closely connected, feeding on each other. The higher the anxiety, the more spouses may isolate from each other, which in turn lowers responsible communication and increases gossip with other people outside the marriage.[205]

One of the dangers of empathy, an important trait, is that it can easily slip into anxious fusion.[206] We care so much that we anxiously lose the big picture. Calmness sets tone. Marital clarity is more important even than empathy, because it brings objectivity and reduces anxiety.[207] How calm and clear are you about your marriage?

CHAPTER 14

Saying No to the Blame Game

Amajor reason why Janice retired was to spend more time with our grandchildren. It is thrilling for us to be with them a couple of times a week. Sometimes our apartment needs a bit of cleaning after a visit by our dear grandchildren. Recently a two-year old grandchild, while visiting, needed Vaseline for dry lips. After applying a bit of Vaseline, Janice thought that she had put the Vaseline out of reach. While Janice was out of the room, our grandchild somehow found the Vaseline and smeared it all over their face, clothes, boots, the wall, and the floor. It took hours to get the stickiness off the floor at our front entrance. Ed had thought that our grandchild was fine, because Ed could see our grandchild quietly playing. Janice was not pleased with the mess, and felt tempted to blame Ed rather than own her part. It took Ed a few hours to own his part. Finally, he apologized for not adequately child-proofing the house, and Janice forgave Ed for blaming her. Giving up blaming is almost like giving up smoking. It may feel impossible, but it can be done, one day at a time.

One of the eight key Bowen concepts is family projection process. This involves the projection of anxiety and conflict onto other family members, particularly in a multigenerational manner. Through the family projection process, some people blame their spouse and some blame themselves. The term *blame* comes from the Greek word *blasphemos*: "evil speaking, slander, to revile, to reproach." What if we said no to cursing and reproaching our spouse? In life, we either bless or curse. Which will it be for you? Blessing is a radical choice in the midst of marital anxiety. Could you ask God to help you become more of a blessing to your spouse? Marital bliss comes through marital blessing.

Married couples often relieve anxiety by projecting their anxiety onto their spouse or others, thereby making them weaker.[208] We can project onto the other spouse the identity of an "identified person positive" (IP+) or an "identified person negative" (IP–). When we project onto our spouse IP+, we pedestalize them, exaggerating their messianic qualities, only to knock them off the pedestal and identify them as IP–. This superior–inferior assessment of our spouse can flip very quickly. The payoff in identifying the other spouse as IP– is a temporary reduction of anxiety.[209] Before we cut off from our spouse or parents, we usually identify them as IP–. They become "the problem". In the more serious cases of cutoff, we roll our eyes, as we contemptuously deny our spouse's essential humanity and worth.

Married couples may immaturely project their anxiety and undifferentiation on their children. The more fused we are to our children, the greater the temptation to put them on a pedestal or see them as the problem. The payoff is a temporary anxiety reduction in our marriages.

In Janice's family, they all admired their father, putting him on a pedestal as the IP+. One of the children became identified as the IP– both in the family and in the school system. The inability to solve the problems associated with this child led the family into a deeper dependence on Christ and prayer than they had previously experienced. No family or marital pain is ever wasted.

By seeing others as the problem in the marriage and family, one doesn't have to work on oneself. It's their fault, isn't it? Such transfer of anxiety involves the projection of one's own feelings of helplessness, weakness, and inadequacy. Without discriminating between feeling and reality, such feelings of helplessness define the person and then become projected onto the other spouse or a third party.[210] Bowen taught that the therapeutic emphasis is to be directed at this helplessness. Through getting help from a coach, the couple discover their strengths and their problem-solving abilities. They are able to move from being passive to becoming marital activists and change-agents. Bowen said that many, before receiving coaching, had seen their marital problems as individual burdens to be endured rather than family problems to be solved: "It is not traumatic action but passive lack of action that is incapacitation."[211] To what degree does your family of origin tend to go passive when faced by challenges?

We sent our three children to public schools, seeking to be salt and light in a broken world. When one of our sons was in Grade 6, public school was no longer working for him; he was being bullied, and the teacher didn't deal with it. We made the painful decision to move our children to a Christian school. We had often said we could not afford a Christian school, but we couldn't afford not to. So we made the sacrifice, breaking through the passivity around our son being bullied.

To break the power of family projection, Bowen usually avoided a relationship with the family member that the family process had already designated as ''sick'' or "the patient."[212] By working with the highest functioning, the most motivated, and the pursuers, Bowen turned the family projection process on its head, thereby bridging marital cutoff. Bowen said that in each family and marriage, there is an active person who gets thing done:

> If there is just one thing for the therapist to do, it is to sup-
> port the family member who motivates the situation.... [W]
> e would now say to support him in whatever direction he
> chooses, no matter how illogical it might seem.[213]

Since you are actually taking time to read this marriage book, perhaps you are the motivated family member that Bowen is describing. By becoming more aware of your family projection process, the tendency to weaken, scapegoat, and cut each other off can be reduced. Who tends to be identified as the IP+s or IP–s in your family system?

CHAPTER 15

The Family that Stays Together

If you will work on your family of origin, you will be amazed at how much your marriage will improve. You can waste your time blaming your spouse. But if you do your personal work, you will have an incredible payoff. You can't change your spouse. You've already tried it. You know it doesn't work. You can't change your family of origin. But you can begin to observe your family and look at patterns. You begin to see what you are doing and how you can shift. Richardson says,

> Few of us like to own up to it, but our own personal emotional maturity is a major part of the difficulty in our relationships; this usually goes back to relationship difficulties with our family of origin…. What is unresolved with our families is likely, in some form, to be unresolved with our adult partner.[214]

The high road to marital growth is through a deeper understanding of the family we were raised in. Both Jesus and Paul reaffirmed Moses' teaching in the Ten Commandments to honour our father and mother. The Good Book teaches that as we honour our sometimes difficult parents, our lives will be longer and better.[215] If we write off our parents and family of origin, it means that we are unusually stuck. It may be tricky to go back, but any work that we do in that area without judging, just going as an observer, can be huge. Even if our family of origin cuts us off, there is always someone, perhaps a distant relative, that you can do family-of-origin work with. If there is someone older who loves to talk about the family, go visit that aunt or that distant cousin and say, "Tell me about the family. I am interested." You will be amazed at the family patterns that go on and on and on. In the Strengthening Marriage Workshop, we taught,

If you want to be healthy in your marriage and nuclear family, then you go back to your family of origin. You don't go back to change them or fix them. You just go back to observe them, and you do it often through questions.... You go back as a scientist, very gently. The more you can get family-of-origin insights, the more breakthroughs you have in your marriage. You can choose to beat yourself up, or you can be grumpy at your family of origin, or you can be objective and say, "This is kind of who we are. It's a bit quirky maybe. But I am going to analyze my family of origin as if I am studying some undiscovered tribe that has these unique behaviour patterns. So, I am just going to observe this and see what I discover." In this way, you can take your findings back to your marriage in a way that will affect your own marriage and nuclear family. That may be a bit hard to believe. You can test it for yourself.[216]

Through careful, observation, the pastoral coach can equip you to bring your family system more alive. You will benefit greatly through examining where you have both come from, and where you might be heading, integrating the past, present, and future. Some couples are so narcissistically absorbed in the anxious present that they have no energy to give to their seemingly irrelevant family-of-origin past. In strengthening a marriage, one does not have to choose between past, present, and future. Remarkably, many couples may make more progress through family-of-origin work than even through going for coaching sessions.[217] Working on your family of origin has a major impact on your marriage for better, for worse.

Too often, we bring with us into our marriage the "baggage" from our families or previous relationships. It is very easy to either cut off or emotionally fuse to one's painful past: "They did this to me; they did that. I'll never forgive them." Clinging to how we were mistreated in the past can steal our possibilities for joy and leave us feeling bitter in our current marriage. Bitterness is often connected with the death of our dreams. The book of Hebrews says that bitterness will defile and harass our most valuable relationships, leaving our hearts hardened and cold (Hebrews 12:15). We are often oblivious to how hardened our hearts have become to our partner. It may feel totally normal. Divorce, said Jesus, is closely connected with hardness of the heart.[218] We harden our hearts to cope with emotional pain. Without realizing it, we may end up exchanging a heart of love for a heart of stone. Hardening of the arteries can be not only a physical problem but also a spiritual and emotional issue. With Ed's successful stent heart surgery, he is particularly keen to avoid "hardening of arteries" in his marriage. As Proverbs 4:23 puts it, "Above all else, guard your heart, for everything you do flows from it." Broken hearts can sometimes become hardened. Where might family-of-origin work help you heal any brokenness in your heart?

Some couples may be reluctant to reconnect with their family of origin, thinking that will stir up trouble. It has been so long since there has been any contact that it may feel like going into a war zone.[219] Some, particularly those who have burned their emotional bridges, wonder if they have any family of origin out there to reconnect with. Others are in contact with their family but at great emotional distance, returning home very infrequently for duty visits.[220] Without coaching, going back to one's family of origin may backfire.[221] Family-of-origin work helps repair the generational damage of emotional distance and cutoff.[222] You will remember how Bowen defined cutoff as the process of separation, isolation, withdrawal, running away, or denying the importance of the parental family. Has there been any running away in your family of origin? Would you like to rediscover the importance of your sometimes painful family?

If you can get a one-on-one relationship with each living person in your extended family, it will help you grow up more than anything you could ever do in life. Bowen encouraged us to do our family-of-origin work as a research project of life. This family-of-origin work by married couples must be done for the sake of self rather than for togetherness.[223] One of the best places for couples to start is with the oldest members of their families.[224] We will never outgrow the need to keep on restoring these multigenerational bridges. One of the best places to learn about the past is with older family members. Contact with both the older and younger generations brings higher marital functioning.[225] Such contact helps build bridges and reverses the patterns of avoidance, blame, withdrawal, and cutoff. Who might you dialogue with in your generational network? Do you have any grandparents still living who might love a visit? Or elderly parents? Or long-lost cousins? Because cutoff instinctively shrinks our definition about who is included as family, Richardson says that it is best to contact all family members rather than a narrow subset.[226]

Married couples are encouraged, when visiting their family members, to look for the generational facts, as facts tell a story about their family's level of differentiation. Family-of-origin work for couples is a fact-finding mission that helps each spouse become more of a self rather than a pseudo-self.[227] It is important when doing family-of-origin research to look for key points where people have left or entered their family. All of us, including married couples, are more emotionally attached and fused to our family of origin than we realize.[228] Rediscovering your family helps you remove your emotional masks in your marriage. God can use family-of-origin work to turn the hearts of the fathers to their children and the hearts of the children to their parents.[229]

Bowen admitted that, as happened with his own parents, this family-of-origin work will not necessarily go smoothly. He had mistaken avoidance and distance from his family as emancipation, but he had unfinished emotional business with them.[230] Bowen's breakthrough happened in 1966 on a home visit when Bowen was able to relate to his family about emotional issues without becoming personally caught in the process. His family of origin's initial angry response was to write Bowen off as crazy, but they eventually came to refer to Bowen by the honorific title of the differentiating one.[231] Would you like to become known in your family as the differentiating one?

Much of the Hird family of origin can be traced to Northern England. Each of the four times we have visited England, we have wanted to visit relatives and close friends, especially in our earlier visits when so many family members were still living. To celebrate our thirtieth wedding anniversary, we flew to Northern England to visit our youngest son, serving then as a youth missionary in Newcastle. Our son detriangled and matured greatly during that year. So did his parents. While in England, Ed reflected on the amazing gift of being married to someone whom you really like to be with. Janice has been that gift to Ed. She has been loyal in supporting the ministry at St. Simon's North Vancouver. That is why Ed dedicated his second book, *Battle for the Soul of Canada*, with gratitude to his dear wife.

The irony of family-of-origin work is that, in connecting with one's past, a person is intentionally stimulating the very painful anxiety that produced the initial family cutoff. Making short visits helps reduce the reactivity so that married couples can be better observers.[232] Nichols encouraged connecting with the most emotionally distant member of the family, which is often the father. Many of us have discovered that the intensity of our need as emotional pursuer of our spouse and children is due in part to unfinished family-of-origin business.[233]

A key to breakthrough with one's family of origin is self-differentiation which involves distinguishing between the thinking, feeling, and emotional family systems. Understanding our own goals helps prevent us from becoming swallowed up in the swirling family emotional whirlpool.[234] Richardson notes that cutoff may increase during times of family deaths as a way of coping with new family triangles.[235] Perhaps this is why Bowen encouraged us to visit our families of origin, to observe and potentially bridge cutoff during these critical life transitions of death, birth, weddings, and holidays. Illnesses and holidays are also natural contexts that provide enough anxiety to ignite the family reactivity.[236] You will not want to use the holiday times to emotionally confront and dump on your family. The key with family-of-origin work is to observe others but work on self, not the other way around.[237] Photographs, language, or memory of history can be helpful in family-of-origin connecting.[238]

There are no quick fixes in family-of-origin work. We have to give up looking for marital cures. Bowen said it takes about four years before family-of-origin patterns can be changed.[239] Ed and Janice are in this for the long haul. We still do foolish things in our marriage. We're just going to keep working on this relationship. We're going to say no to the quick fix. Quick fixes make it worse. Don't go for the sudden solution in your marriage. Keep working on your marriage, for better, for worse.

Speaking of quick, both Ed and Janice are sometimes unexpectedly quicker or slower than the other. In forty years of marriage, we have irritated each other many times by keeping the other person waiting. Neither of us likes being late for appointments. Sometimes we can be like the irresistible force and the unmovable object. At times, we both struggle with impatience. In doing our family-of-origin work, we have realized that this is a common family pattern throughout all the generations. Our families have a go-getter intensity that is very good for getting jobs done quickly, but it can sometimes be painful for others in the wider family to keep up. Our speed can make us come across as insensitive, even pushy. People have been known to sometimes hide from us or passively resist us when we hurry. Might you too need to slow down and be more patient as you work on your family-of-origin patterns?

One of the most helpful ways for married couples to do family-of-origin work is to map out their family genogram. Richardson says that "if you have ever drawn your own family diagram or genogram, you know that the act itself is helpful. It may be the first step in getting more emotional distance from your family."[240] You can Google "family systems genogram" to see a picture of what this family road map looks like, and how to draw your family's genogram. We would also recommend Ron Richardson's classic book *Family Ties that Bind* which gives many illustrations of genograms and how to draw them.[241]

You will remember Linda and Lloyd, who remarried each other after being divorced for six years. While attending our Strengthening Marriage Workshop, they both did genograms, which they found insightful for better understanding their family patterns. Emotional cutoff was a common theme on both sides of their family. While having marriage coaching, Linda and Lloyd expressed the desire that their daughter, Lucy, would marry her partner Larry. Ed said to Linda, "Have you ever apologized to your daughter for divorcing Lloyd?" Linda said, "No, I never thought of that." Linda apologized to Lucy. Then Lucy phoned Ed, asking him to take her wedding. Is there anyone in your family of origin that you might consider forgiving or apologizing to?

CHAPTER 16

Triangles and Strengthening Marriages

nother key to reducing emotional cutoff is through observing marital triangles, usually made up of the two spouses and one other person. Sometimes a triangle involves one of the spouses and two other people. Bowen's concept of a triangle in marriage is different than the common "love triangle" concept of a lover outside the couple. When first introduced to the concept of triangles by his doctoral adviser Paddy Ducklow, Ed found himself resistant. Over time, he started to see its significance. Once you look for triangles in marriages, you'll find them everywhere.[242] Triangles exist in all relationships. Triangles are the smallest stable emotional unit. They are the cement that integrates the other seven Bowen concepts into one unified theoretical basis.

Marital coaching is always triangular in nature, if only because it involves the pastor or therapist, but more often because it includes the child or in-laws. Bowen remarkably stated that most of his Family Systems learnings came from studying triangles. He did not personally like the term *triangle*, as it was mathematical rather than biological. But he stuck with it for lack of a better biological term. Structured marital patterns tend to repeat in triangles.[243]

Bowen's most important family-of-origin breakthrough was that he was able to detriangle from his parents. The solution to triangling is detriangling oneself. Staying out of triangles by stepping back emotionally increases our ability to see the family emotional system. Observing triangles enables us to realize when we are being emotionally reactive rather than thoughtfully responsive. Controlling such reactivity is at the heart of detriangling. One's parents may triangulate behind "we-ness" and remain hidden from the bid for re-connection.[244] Activating one's family's triangles is key to bringing detriangulation. Even if one's direct ancestor is dead, the family triangles can still be activated through visiting cousins. Your best family-of-origin work happens when you start noticing your family triangles.

You may be finding the triangle concept a bit overwhelming, as we did initially. We encourage you to give it some time to sink in, because when you start seeing triangles in your family, it will greatly improve your marriage. Don't give up. You have made it this far in the book. Detriangling significantly reduces marital cutoff. This is because emotional cutoff is a triangular, not a solitary, activity.[245] The more that you begin to see the previously invisible triangles in your family, the less likely you will be to take things personally and blame your spouse.[246]

The two-person dyad of the married couple is inherently unstable, especially during times of anxiety. The dyad (a husband and a wife) naturally draw in and triangulate to a third party.[247] Many married couples find intimacy painful because of the fused loss of self, and they avoid dyadic intimacy by quickly triangling with a third party.[248] Such triangulation in a married couple creates an appearance of calmness because the anxiety is being transferred to the third party of the triangle.[249] Have you observed pseudo-calmness in your family, when everyone pretends nothing is wrong? Like crabs at the beach, triangles are hiding under every rock, just waiting to be uncovered. Once you start noticing hidden triangles in your family, it can actually become fun, as you learn so much more about your marriage and family.

Emotional distance between the married couple brings one spouse closer to the third party in the triangle. Some people who do not wish to work on self or their own part in a relationship may choose triangulation as a convenient substitute.[250] Married couples can triangulate in many ways, such as by gossiping with others about the relationship or by discussing politics, TV, etc., anything that avoids dealing with self, other, and the relationship. Triangulation can be a way of hiding from marital intimacy.

In the three churches that we have served in the past thirty-seven years, we have met many triangled couples who hide in plain sight from each other. With the rise of the Internet, many spouses have gone missing in action, caught up in Internet gambling, pornography, or video gaming. It is remarkable how many new ways we have invented to hide from authentic relationship. How much hiding have you observed in your family of origin?

There is a close connection between triangles and self-differentiation. Bowen held that differentiation of self takes place only in a triangle. The most effective method of differentiation was in the triangle consisting of the two closest family members (the two spouses) and the coach.[251] The lower the differentiation of the married couple, the more active the triangles will be in funnelling anxiety. Anxiety moves around the triangles of the family.[252] The presence of the third party, such as a new baby, sometimes calms the marital dyad but at other times anxiously destabilizes it because of the enormous energy investment needed.

Anxiety is the major shaper of triangular activity. Triangles spread the anxiety more widely, therefore "protecting" the marital dyad from emotionally overheating and burning out. Triangulating spouses target less secure individuals in their projecting anxiety onto them.[253] Nichols said that triangles can be identified by observing whom the spouse goes to when they emotionally distance from their spouse. Who do you go to when you are emotionally distancing from your spouse?

Triangles tend to be repetitive, reactive, predictable, and automatic.[254] Emotional triangles (made up of three people, often the parents and the child) are more stable, flexible, and able to contain anxiety than with the married couple. When triangles are overwhelmed by anxiety, they interlock with other triangles in order to share the anxious load. Kerr and Bowen taught that with two parents and two children, you already have four triangles. The addition of one more child brings you to ten triangles just in one nuclear family. The higher the anxiety of the married couple, the greater the number of interlocking triangles formed.[255] Variables affecting the triangles are gender, birth order, family patterns, and key multigenerational events.[256] One cannot positively affect triangulation in married couples by trying to change other people in their triangle. Trying to change others in the marital triangle is likely to reinforce the very aspects you wish to change.[257]

When Janice was younger, she would phone and talk to Ed's mother about how to change Ed and the children. His mom would listen carefully and give Janice good advice, helping her to detriangle in her sometimes-fused marriage relationship. Janice would usually feel less anxious and more hopeful after being in her mother-in-law's presence.

Presence changes everything, including our marital triangles. The Bible teaches over 200 times about the importance of presence. King David shared in the bread of the Presence on the table of the Presence.[258] King Josiah renewed the covenant in the presence of the Lord.[259] The epitaph on both Ed's mom's and grandmother's gravestones, "Joyful in His Presence," refers to Psalm 16:11.[260] The healthiest marriages have covenantal joy both in each other's presence and in His presence.

Titelman said there are many forms that detriangling takes: expressing neutrality-objectivity, humour, reversal, systems questioning, and avoiding fusion. Detriangling is closely linked to self-differentiating. Ironically, detriangulation is facilitated by the pastoral coach creating "a new triangle, a therapeutic one" with the couple.[261] Detriangulation is not about manipulating and controlling the married couple but rather about setting healthy boundaries so that one is not manipulated and controlled by others.[262] Are you currently able to say no to manipulation and control? Detriangling can help you be healthier when pressured by others.

Objectivity and neutrality are both key for a spouse to detriangle from their spouse. Neutrality is key to reducing marital polarization. Bowen defined emotional neutrality as the ability to be in the presence of disharmony without taking sides. Staying neutral and refusing to take sides with either spouse is the "central, most challenging task" and first priority for the pastoral coach.[263] Marital coaching is particularly vulnerable to getting caught in triangles. There is no formula for quick-fix neutrality. To be charmed or angered neutralizes our neutrality. We need to resist and repent of the temptation to "read other people's minds". Giving marital advice is one way of unhelpfully taking a side.[264] Detriangulating may look like the pastoral coach is doing nothing, when all the while they are balancing on a shaky high wire. In our activist, technique-oriented western society, "doing nothing" as a way of strengthening marriages doesn't look impressive.

Sometimes a spouse or pastoral coach may try to detriangulate prematurely before they have become objectively neutral themselves. Such attempts will usually go badly.[265] It is better to just keep in touch and wait until the anxiety level has moderated before attempting detriangulation. No one is immune from being triangled, and from triangling others.[266] Bowen insightfully noted,

> No one ever stays outside, but a knowledge of triangles makes it possible to get outside on one's own initiative while staying emotionally in contact with the family.[267]

Triangulated marital conflict is closely connected with secrecy and gossip. Such triangular marital processes have their rules about "keeping gossip secret." Bowen stated that relationships can become distant and hostile when there are secrets.[268] Marital secrets have negative effects in the next generation. Part of detriangling and growing up is letting go of secret gossip.[269] As Alcoholics Anonymous puts it, we are as sick as our secrets. What kind of secrets are normal in your family triangles? Would you like to break the power of secrecy, replacing it with more openness and transparency in your marriage?

One of the most memorable examples of triangulation and detriangling is the biblical story of Joseph and his eleven brothers. After being rejected by his brothers, Joseph later became in charge of Egypt. In an unforgettable expression of detriangling, Joseph forgave his brothers with tears, saying in Genesis 50:20, "You intended to harm me but, God intended it for good to accomplish what is now being done, the saving of many lives."

CHAPTER 17

Keys to Relationship Breakthrough

Many of us have been disillusioned by institutions but lack anything solid with which to replace them. People used to have great respect for institutions such as major department stores, schools, churches, police, and military. Even marriage as an institution can become suspect to our jaded eyes. What is missing in most marriages today, said R. Paul Stevens, is what the Bible identifies as the heart of marriage: a covenant.[270] What is a covenant, you may ask? A covenant is a pledge, a vow, a promise made in the presence of God. Marriage as covenant helps recover our respect for the historic roots of marriage. Covenantal thinking enables us become more self-differentiated and objective in our marriages. Through embracing the marriage covenant, we become less emotionally fused and more guided by our core principles and beliefs. We live in a society that emphasizes rights more than responsibilities, an out-of-balance emphasis that does not help married couples.[271] Covenantal thinking helps us balance the dance of both rights and responsibilities in our marriage relationship. Many couples have discovered through covenant thinking that God is good, faithful and kind to them. God as covenant-maker rescues, renews, forgives, and heals, taking what is broken and making it whole. Would you like to experience the marriage benefits of covenant thinking?

Ever since becoming a Christian in 1972 and developing an unshakable hunger for Bible reading, Ed has been fascinated with the meaning of marriage. Reading Matthew 19:6 (What God has joined together, let no one put asunder), he was shocked to discover that God invented marriage. God actually joins a husband and wife together as one flesh in the marriage covenant. Because God believes in it, therefore marriages are worth fighting for and investing in. Up to that point, Ed had held the unoriginal view that marriage was just a piece of paper, a merely human invention. He had never even heard of marriage being a covenant.

He remembers sharing with Janice on their first date in 1975 about his fascination with the biblical theology of "one flesh" marriage. She found Ed somewhat overwhelming and told him that she wasn't ready to commit, as she had just broken up with her fiancé. Forty years later, Janice and Ed are still together, leading Strengthening Marriage Workshops locally and in international settings.

While completing his Master of Divinity degree, Ed wrote an essay on the theology of marriage, with a strong emphasis on covenant. Ed concluded the essay by writing his own marriage ceremony and inviting his liturgy professor, Bill Adams, to his wedding. Fortunately, his professor liked the wedding service and gave Ed a good mark. Even then, back in 1977, Ed's passion for marriage was rooted in covenant when he wrote the following for the wedding service:

> For the Christian, marriage is a covenant of faith and trust between a man and woman, a covenant grounded in their shared commitment to Jesus Christ as Lord…. A wedding is the celebration of the highest we know in human love. It is a celebration of a couple coming to the point where they are truly willing to become one flesh in body, mind and spirit…. Question of Intent: Edward (Janice), will you have Janice (Edward) to be your wedded wife (husband), to live together in the covenant of faith, hope, and love that is offered to you in Jesus Christ…. Janice and Edward, you may now seal this covenant with a kiss…. Almighty God, look graciously, we pray, on Janice and Edward and on all whom you make to be one flesh in holy marriage.[272]

Covenant is one of the most important themes in the whole of the Scriptures. The term *covenant* is rarely used in contemporary English. *To be as good as your word* is a modern example of covenantal language. In the past twenty-five years, there has been a renaissance of interest in covenant theology. It is once again being seen as foundational to biblical literature, even as an overarching theme and key to unlocking the biblical epic story. Meredith Kline said that the discovery of the covenant connection with ancient Near Eastern treaties is more important than even the unearthing of the Dead Sea Scrolls.[273]

The rabbis regarded the Jewish marriage service as reflecting the main features of God's covenant with Israel at Mount Sinai. God's covenants with Israel were often described as marriage covenants.[274] Everything that God has done, is doing, and will do through our biblical heritage comes out of his covenants. This is why recovery of marriage as covenant is so vital in strengthening marriages and bridging emotional cutoff. Before reading this book, did you see marriage as a covenant relationship?

The problem with covenants is that we tend to break them, even in marriage. Genesis 17:14 clearly connects the breaking of covenant with cutoff. In the midst of the idolatry and immorality of Romans 1, Paul identifies us as covenant-breakers (verse 31).[275] The good news is that Christ's covenant-keeping atones for our covenant-breaking.

You may have noticed that the phrase "In the name of the Father and of the Son and of the Holy Spirit" is used in many weddings. Does the Holy Trinity have anything to do with having a better marriage? Marital covenant love is rooted in the Trinitarian love of the Father, Son, and Spirit before the creation of the world.[276] We love because the triune God first loved us. We as the beloved of God are accepted in the Beloved Son.[277] Beloved means deeply loved. Marriage is meant to reflect the loving unity among the Father, Son, and Holy Spirit. Even though God the Father, the Son, and the Holy Spirit are one God, they are the most self-differentiated beings in the cosmos. Each of them, while one, has their own role and personality. If that is true for God, that can be true for us in our marriage. The marriage covenant is also about unity without absorption. Covenant love not only accepts our unique marital and family differences but actually celebrates them as strengths. Our differences are meant to be signs of God's gracious covenant presence. The God-given beauty of our spouse disappears when we force them to become us. Stieglitz notably says that opposites attract until they are married, and then they often fuss with and try to fix each other.[278] Self-differentiation and covenant love go hand and hand in a healthy marriage. We covenantally love our spouse enough to celebrate them being themselves. Covenant love liberates. It is for covenantal freedom that Christ sets us free.[279] Would you like to experience more of this covenantal freedom in your relationship?

The Secrets of Leaving and Cleaving

Commitment, says Stevens, is a big word today, but *covenant* is a bigger word.[280] Couples who believe their marriage is something God desires are more likely to act and think in ways that protect their marriage. How might it revolutionize our marriages if we rediscover the biblical teaching in Hebrews 13:4 that the marriage bed is sacred? It is the marriage bed that is sacred rather than the substitutes. As *The Message* translation puts it, "Honour marriage and guard the sacredness of sexual intimacy between husband and wife."[281] Physical intimacy outside of the marriage bed brings unhealthy fusion and confusion to anyone involved. The good news is that we can receive forgiveness and cleansing as we choose to forsake all others. Would you like to ask God to release you from any previous attachments so that you can fully thrive in your marriage?

As an Anglican priest/presbyter, Ed values the great riches in the *Book of Common Prayer* marriage liturgy, which speaks of the marriage covenant as "an honourable estate, instituted of God in the time of man's innocency." The Anglican prayer book also speaks about performing and keeping the vow and covenant made by the couple.[282] Marriage, for both Jews and Christians, is rooted in the covenantal cleaving and leaving of the first marriage in Genesis 2. By quoting Genesis 2:24 in Matthew 19:5, Jesus reaffirms that marriage is essentially covenantal. The purpose of the marriage covenant, says Stevens, is to belong, to bless and to be blessed.[283] The term *bless* is covenantal, coming from the Old English word *blod* (consecrated with blood). There is no greater covenantal blessing than Jesus lovingly shedding his blood on the cross for us.

Covenant love is stronger than all the forces of emotional cutoff. We know women who have stayed faithfully with husbands who were unfaithful to the marriage covenant. The betrayal was very hard for these women, but their covenant love won their husbands back to them after many years of cutoff. Staying faithful, however, does not mean that one's spouse will always return and change.

Marriage is both a social contract and a covenant partnership. To reduce one of the most fundamental building blocks of society to a mere contract is to decrease its covenantal power. God as covenant maker remains faithful to His covenant even when we are not faithful. Marital cutoff is a breaking of covenant, breaking of faith.[284] Because all the couples in our Strengthening Marriage Workshop were divorced and remarried, they all understood the deep pain of covenant breakdown and also the joy of covenant restoration in their second marriages. Linda and Lloyd, who attended the Marriage Workshop, were unique in being divorced for six years and then remarried to the same person. We still marvel at the miraculous transformation of their marriage.

The marriage covenant is a three-fold cord. Have you ever tried to weave together just two strands of rope? It can't be done! The two strands can be wound around each other—twisted together—but they soon come unravelled. Ecclesiastes 4:12 tells us that "a three-fold cord is not quickly broken." It takes three strands to braid a strong, lasting covenant marriage. The third cord in a marriage is meant to be the person of Jesus Christ. Ed and Janice's mutual relationship with Jesus Christ has caused them many times to choose covenantal forgiveness. Christ-centredness is the distinguishing mark of covenantal marriage. Would you like Christ to be the centre of your marriage, for better, for worse? This may be a new thought for you that you will need time to process.

Have you ever watched the Netflix hit series *The Crown* which tells the fascinating story of Queen Elizabeth's adventures and challenges over the past sixty years? We were moved by Queen Elizabeth's private meetings with Billy Graham where she drew closer to Christ. God saved the Queen. This Christ-centeredness enabled the Queen to forgive her uncle, the former King Edward VIII, for his underhandedly seeking appeasement (or worse) with the Nazis. Initially she had told Edward: "There is no possibility of me forgiving you." Queen Elizabeth went on through the series to forgive many people again and again, including Princess Margaret, Jacqueline Kennedy, and especially her husband Prince Philip to whom she has been married for over seventy years.

At the heart of the marriage covenant is unconditional commitment, as in "I pledge you/give thee my troth." The Anglican prayer book uses *troth* to define the wedding vows at the core of the marriage service. *Troth*, as in betrothal, is an Old English term for truth, faithfulness, loyalty, and honesty. We pledge "to have and to hold from this day forward, for better for worse, for richer for poorer, in sickness and health, to love and to cherish, till death do us part." Love is stronger than death itself. [285] *The Book of Common Prayer* richly says, "Then shall they give their troth to each other… and thereto I give thee my troth." Many contemporary marriage liturgies now use the phrase "vow" as an equivalent of troth. Our commitment to covenant faithfulness is a commitment to troth, to marital truth. It takes courage to share your truth vulnerably with your spouse. Sharing our troth/truth helps us move from the pseudo-self of dating to the true self of an authentic, transparent marriage. Would you like to remove your mask through embracing the truth? It is the truth that sets your marriage free. Have you been hiding your truth, your troth, from your spouse? What truth do you need to gently share with your beloved in a way that they can hear? Ed's truth is that he comes alive in Janice's presence, particularly when he is willing to listen to and accept her wisdom. Janice's truth is that she loves to be with Ed as a companion, especially when he listens to her and helps her with her many projects.

Covenant marriage, if strong and persevering, can survive setbacks, selfishness, and sabotage. Stevens calls the marriage covenant a net between two trapeze artists, swinging back and forth. [286] The Bible gives couples the Spirit-filled strength to finish well as they covenantally commit not only to the present moment but, more importantly, to the unknown future, for better or for worse. To disregard the marriage covenant is to lose the significance of commitment and fidelity, the surrender of one's own will to the cause of the other spouse. [287] Would you like to make a covenant commitment to finishing well in your marriage, till death do you part?

Covenant love is a key protection against marital despair and abandonment. Safety, grounded in covenant love, facilitates marital intimacy. How secure is your spouse that you will be there for them, for better or for worse, that you will defend them, come what may? Do they know that you have their back? Janice's loyalty has enabled Ed to thrive in an often-challenging ministry context. How loyal are you to your spouse when life is tough? At the heart of the marriage covenant promise is the intention to commit to the health of the marriage "till death do us part." Adultery and dishonesty are shattering to covenant trust, a trust grounded in the forsaking of all others. Marital infidelity is a form of covenantal cutoff that may reflect generational patterns. Adultery, while devastating, does not preclude marital reconciliation. Ed has been privileged to help a number of couples recover from the traumatic pain of adultery. Has there been any adultery in the past generations of your family? The good news is that you can pray and ask God to set you free from strongholds of sexual infidelity in past generations.

There are good reasons why covenant marriage vows include the phrase "in sickness and in health." One of the most difficult setbacks Ed and Janice ever faced was when, due to a rare viral throat infection, Ed lost his voice for eighteen months in the first year of his ordination. The doctors diagnosed it as spasmodic dysphonia. This voice disorder causes the vocal chords to over-adduct (over-shut) on a spasmodic or intermittent basis, cutting off words or parts of sentences as you're trying to talk. His GP told him he would never preach again. Janice was pregnant with their first child. After going to ten specialists, Ed was told to step down from ministry, or he might never regain his voice. Ed was shocked to discover that he had no long-term disability insurance. So we began to live out the marriage vow "for richer or poorer."

Around that time, we learned that God would meet our needs if we put him first and tithed our first 10 percent. As we had no income, we figured that 10 percent of nothing was possible. Miraculously God met our needs for the next year until Ed's voice was restored through throat surgery and he was able to serve as the assistant priest at St. Matthew's Abbotsford. It was covenant love and faithfulness that enabled our marriage to thrive in those very difficult times. Covenant marriage is never only about itself but rather is about a marital calling to love the other, be it the wider family, the church family, or the community.

Covenant renewal is at the heart of marriage renewal. Entering into a covenant, whether with our spouse or with God, must not be half-hearted but rather with all our heart and soul.[288] Many people have never realized that the command to whole-heartedly love your neighbour as yourself includes the love of one's spouse.[289] Are you currently more half-hearted or whole-hearted in your marriage? What might you like to do about that, for better, for worse?

Covenant love doesn't trap us in our past but rather moves us toward our sometimes strange and exciting future. The genuinely other can be strange to us. The other sex will always be different from you and see things in a different way. Is it okay with you for the other sex to be genuinely other, to not be the same as you? Sometimes their insights may feel very strange. Marriage is a covenant pilgrimage, moving hand in hand with our sometimes "strange" spouse toward our often unknown future.[290] Covenant love is about being chosen in our uniqueness. What if you celebrated your spouse's very different temperament? Most of us are far more attracted to sameness than we would readily admit. Celebrating strangeness and covenantal otherness is key to marital intimacy. Are you willing to embrace some of the strange aspects of your beloved spouse? Most geniuses and creative people are a bit strange, at least until you get used to them. Are you willing to become more curious about the "otherness" of your "strange" spouse? What if that initial strangeness became the key to your mutual creative future? What if you intentionally encouraged your spouse to be more self-differentiated, to not be you, even if that feels strange?

By reducing our emotional fusion and celebrating covenantal otherness, we find greater gender equality with our spouse. Emotional fusion leads to spouses unequally giving up self or taking self from each other. Have you ever seen couples do that—allow themselves to be dominated, to be a doormat to their spouse? In a lot of cultures, that is fairly normal; it is all that they know. In patriarchal cultures, the woman is often the doormat, and in matriarchal cultures sometimes the man is the doormat. Now and then it flips back and forth in a marriage, where we are either the dominant person or give up self.

Self-differentiation is key to embracing gender equality and ending the gender war. Equality doesn't mean sameness. it means mutually moving in your different giftings because you have diverse gifts that complement each other in your marriage. Self-differentiated spouses are so much more fun to be around, for better, for worse.

Due to the premature death of numerous men in her family, Janice's mom was raised with the view that men are more special than women. So the men were unequally catered to in all instances. When Janice was nine, her mom told her that she had hoped that Janice would be a boy. Through prayer ministry, Janice was able to forgive her mother and embrace the gift of her femininity. The strongholds of rejection and resentment no longer controlled her. By the time her mother passed away from cancer, there had been a deep reconciliation with her mom, who apologized in tears to her. This embracing of gender equality has enabled Janice to move more freely in her unique giftings as a woman, including overcoming her fear of public speaking and giving hugs. Does it surprise you to realize that the Bible advocates for gender equality while affirming our gender uniqueness?

The Covenantal Marriage of Ephesians 5

Both Ephesians 5 and the parallel passage Colossians 3 express the Apostle Paul's life-changing covenantal view of marriage. There is no more extensive teaching on marriage in the Bible than in Ephesians 5. Paul shows men a Spirit-filled way to be Christ-like to their wives in a way that is not harsh or enslaving.[291] The biblical concepts of headship and submission can be understood only in light of the mutual submission in Ephesians 5:21: "Submit to one another out of reverence for Christ." Thomas Neufeld and Frank Thielman observed that mutual submission is rooted in being filled with the Holy Spirit. Mutual submission is nothing less than charismatic, Spirit-filled activity.[292] Where the Spirit of the Lord is, there is freedom.[293] Mutual submission is a freely chosen act of self-differentiation. Only the truly free can actually mutually submit to their spouse. How often have we quenched, resisted, grieved, vexed, and even lied to the Holy Spirit as we refuse to practise mutual marital surrender?

Dr. E. Stanley Jones, founder of the United Christian Ashram, once said that "there can be no love between a husband and wife unless there is mutual self-surrender. Love simply cannot spring up without that self-surrender to each other. If either withholds the self, love cannot exist."

A man and his wife were having painful marriage difficulties. The wife went away to a Christian Ashram retreat and surrendered her marriage to the Lord. When she returned home, her husband said to her, "Well, Miss High and Mighty, what did you learn at the Ashram?" She replied, "I've learned that I've been the cause of all our troubles." She got up from her chair, came around beside him and knelt, folded her hands, and said, "Please forgive me. I'm the cause of all our troubles."

At that moment, her husband nearly upset the kitchen table while getting down on his knees beside her. He blurted out, "You're not the cause of all our troubles—I am." There they met each other—and God. Each surrendered to Jesus; then they surrendered to each other and were free. Now this couple, instead of continually criticizing each other, are one in love and forgiveness.[294]

Mutual submission cannot be done in the flesh, in our own human effort. It needs to be done charismatically and covenantally in the power of the Holy Spirit. Both Ephesians 5:19–20 and Colossians 3:16 root marriage in Spirit-filled song. What music did you have at your wedding? Every marriage needs a heart song, a radical unshakable dream. Our dreams or core beliefs are at the heart of our marriage adventure. Marital cutoff is often connected to broken dreams and visions. Bowen said, "That a man dreams is a scientific fact, but what he dreams is not necessarily a fact."[295] Our dreams need to be more than just nice words spoken by our pseudo-self, but rather rooted in our self-chosen principles for living our lives. The marriage covenant, as mentioned, is rooted in troth, speaking and living our truth in this "for better, for worse" life. The most self-differentiated people are the most full of troth, or truthful. When our spouse cannot trust a word that we say, emotional cutoff is just around the corner. Covenant-keeping requires that our yes be a yes, our troth be true. What is your marriage's heart song to which you are being called to say yes? Is there room in your heart for your spouse, perhaps even for God?

In our society, the terms *headship* and *submission* are often instantly misunderstood and dismissed. Stott said that "almost nothing is calculated to arouse more angry protests."[296] Williamson admitted that "these verses are the hardest to understand in the Letter to the Ephesians and cause many people to cringe."[297] A defensiveness around these two concepts does not help bring marital transformation. To flippantly dismiss these concepts is to unintentionally weaken our commitment to the final authority of Holy Scripture. We cannot just wish that the Bible had omitted these embarrassing terms. Rather we must live in the dynamic tension and awkwardness of these important and often confusing insights. Because the Bible is always reliably true, the challenge is to understand its contextual meaning. Avoiding conflict by emotionally cutting ourselves off from this challenging passage only makes matters worse. Nothing, said Neufeld, is to be gained by obscuring the evident difficulties of the text.[298]

Most people nowadays would agree conceptually to the notion of mutual submission. It seems so kind, and even Canadian. F.F. Bruce insightfully said that it is easier to pay lip service to the duty of mutual submission than to practise it.[299] Through mutual submission, the dividing wall of gender hostility becomes torn down. In a world enslaved by selfishly taking and keeping, marital discipleship is about mutually submitting through radically giving and receiving. Our self-centredness is the death of relationship. Mutual submission is the way of relational resurrection, for better, for worse.

Mutual submission is about putting on Christ and living out our baptismal covenant in which there is differentiated unity, neither Jew nor Greek, slave nor free, male nor female (Galatians 3:28–29). What if we both stop blaming the other gender or putting them on the pedestal? Mutual submission bridges emotional cutoff as it affirms that in the Lord, woman is not independent of man, nor is man independent of woman (1 Corinthians 11:11–12). Marriage is a three-legged race, for better, for worse. Independently running ahead of one's spouse causes both to stumble. In marriage, we become emotionally and spiritually connected almost like Siamese twins. Are you ever tempted to impatiently tell your spouse to hurry up? Ed has been working on his impatience for the past forty years of marriage? It seems to be a family-of-origin issue. Ed has been known to often pray "God, give me patience right now." Does your impatience with your spouse ever backfire on you? We need each other more than we often want to admit. We are stronger together. As Spirit-filled marriage partners, we rejoice that as woman came from man so also man is born of woman.

What might our marriages look like if we detriangled from the angry rhetoric that often goes on between men and women? Many spouses are trapped in the "stinking thinking" that they are doing much more than their partner, who doesn't care enough to change. What if men genuinely repented for ways that they have not been living out the covenant love and mutual submission spoken of in Ephesians 5? What if men led the way in humbly turning from selfishness in their marriages?

Ephesians 5:21 is the linchpin for understanding how we live out covenantal relationships. It is providential that vs. 22 lacks a verb, because otherwise we could imagine someone arguing that the verb for submission in vs. 22 has a totally different meaning in the Greek than the verb for submission in vs. 21.[300] Mutual submission between a husband and wife is a radical form of costly love.

Ed and Janice practised mutual submission during the difficult decision to sell their townhouse in the spring of 2017. Initially Ed was resistant to relocating, but as we shared and prayed together, Ed submitted to the wisdom of this action. When Ed suddenly agreed, he moved into his high-energy mode. Then Janice became nervous because it started to feel very real. So she chose to mutually submit and work with Ed in preparing the townhouse for sale. Ed had a strong sense that there was a certain window of opportunity to make a sale. Our mutual submitting caused us to work as a great team in the successful sale within the needed time frame.

In contrast to the commands to children and slaves, Paul does not tell wives to obey their husbands. To love, honour, and *obey* is not found in the Bible. It is notable, said Stott, that the word *exousia* (authority) was not used once in the passage.[301] Headship is not about authority, but rather about service. It is interesting how we are often instinctively drawn toward how we should be treated better by our spouse. Yet the energy of the Ephesians passage is in the opposite direction. It is about going the second mile for one's spouse. The wider passage of Ephesians 5:21–32 is about a husband sacrificing himself through the power of the Holy Spirit for his wife. Ed remembers being in the living room of a Christian couple who were about to split up. Intuitively Ed felt led to read the Ephesians 5 passage. The husband said to Ed, "That's what's wrong with our marriage. She's not practising Ephesians 5." Often, we are tempted to blame others rather than face our part in the Ephesians 5 challenge. We are grateful that this couple ended up going to a Christian clinical counsellor and had their marriage restored in a way that has given hope to many other couples.

The Bible teaches that when our first parents rebelled against God, in Genesis 3, even our marriages became out of kilter. In the Garden of Eden, our first ancestors were originally equal and self-differentiated. Men, after the fall, dominated women, taking self from them. The good news is that because of what Jesus did for us on the cross, we as new creations in Christ have become a new covenant people. Even our marriages can become new in Christ's love. As Stott put it, the new creation in Christ frees us from the distortions between the sexes caused by the fall.[302] Would you like to turn away from controlling and taking self from your partner? What might that look like, for better, for worse?

In the 1970s sitcom *All in the Family,* Archie Bunker often told his wife, Edith, to put a sock in it. He was stating that she wasn't allowed to have her own opinion. Putting wives down has nothing to do with the headship spoken about in both Ephesians 5 and 1 Corinthians 11. Headship is not about who "wears the pants in the family" or who is in charge. Some have unsuccessfully tried to make a case for the Greek word *kephale* (headship) as meaning "the source of a river." Headship is best understood in light of Jesus Christ's humble service in Philippians Chapter 2:1–11.[303] Marital headship is about making oneself nothing and taking the very nature of a servant, even to the foot of the cross, what Family Systems Theory calls "making yourself small."[304] The more self-differentiated we are, the more we are willing to make ourselves small in our marriages. Authentic marital repentance requires that we make ourselves small, admitting that we were wrong and making amends to our spouse. Making ourselves small is about repenting of the pride of our heart.[305] Could marital headship in part be about men reducing their marital overfunctioning, which causes their wives to underfunction and emotionally cutoff? Could marital headship be about men being the self-differentiated catalyst that chooses to remain non-anxiously present to one's wife even in times of potential marital sabotage?

Because the Bible, while paradoxical, does not ultimately contradict itself, marital headship cannot be about lording one's authority (*katexousiazousin*) over another. Rather, marital headship must be about our willingness to become the *doulous*—servant/slave—of all. Jesus taught in Mark 10:45 that the Son of Man came not to be served but to serve and give His life as a ransom for many. Marital headship is a call to Christ-like covenant servanthood, to differentiating enough to wash one another's feet like Christ did. Imagine what the full extent of Jesus' love (John 13:1) might do to strengthen our marriages. Marital headship can best be understood as Christ-likeness, as imitating Christ, as sacrificial *agape* love for one's wife, by giving up oneself for her as Christ did for his bride. What might foot washing look like in your marriage, for better, for worse?

Ed lives out headship in his marriage by doing dishes, helping make dinner, vacuuming when requested, and in moving house to be near our parents. Headship is about sacrificial love till death do us part. The covenantal image of the bridegroom and bride in Ephesians 5 is meant to be a profound expression of liberating love, not coercive domination. As Stott stated, "What stands out in Paul's development of the theme is the steadfastness of the heavenly Bridegroom's covenant love for his bride."[306]

The hippie movement spoke freely about love and peace in the 1967 Summer of Love in which 100,000+ youth came to San Francisco. But such talk of love too often ended in gender exploitation and disillusionment. Without clarity, *love* becomes a meaningless word, used to manipulate one's partner. Once burned, twice shy. "What's love got to do with it?" sang Tina Turner. So often in marriage, we talk a good talk but live our lives as marital hypocrites. Many of you reading this book may have been deeply hurt by people whose pseudo-self talked a good talk before breaking your heart. It can be hard to try again. It may be hard to believe that God still has a truly loving person waiting for you, for better, for worse, to love and to cherish you.

The Greek term *agape* used in Ephesians 5 is a rich word for covenant love.[307] As Stott said, the Stoics also taught their husbands to love, but only with a *phileo* brotherly love. Agape marital love is rooted first and foremost in the cross of Christ. This is the love that God showed in giving up his only Son as a sacrifice. Harold Hoehner noted, "[T]his exhortation to husbands to love their wives is unique. It is not found in the Old Testament, rabbinic literature, or in the household codes of the Greco-Roman era."[308]

It is hard for us to comprehend how countercultural Paul's message would have been to Greco-Roman husbands who were used to looking to mistresses and concubines for their erotic desires:

> [T]he typical Hellenistic view is represented by Pseudo-Demosthenes (fourth century BC): "We have wives to bear us children, concubines for the daily care of our persons, mistresses we keep for the sake of our pleasure."[309]

Paul challenged husbands four times in Ephesians 5 to love their wives. Why did Paul keep repeating himself? Because he wanted men to get this one. Showing covenantal Christ-like love to one's wife is not optional.[310] The most self-differentiated husbands are the most loving. In contrast, Paul never asked the wives to love their husbands, perhaps because they were already doing that. The wife's love for her husband seems to be the last thing that dies in a marriage. Instead Paul encouraged the wives in vs. 33 to respect their husbands, one of the more challenging and vital callings for wives in their marriage covenant. Respecting one's husband's core self, rather than the pseudo-self of the dating scene, is at the heart of lasting intimacy. Some women have been heard to say "I will respect him when he deserves it." Don't wait until your husband deserves respect. The term *deserve* comes from the Latin *deservire*, which means to serve well, to earn, to merit something. What if you showed your husband the grace and favour that he hasn't earned? The Bible challenges wives to respect their husbands by digging for their husband's strengths in the sea of his weaknesses.[311] You can revolutionize your marriage if you become a radical respecter of your husband. Covenantal respect gives your husband the desire to serve you well. Is this a new thought for you? Did your mother intentionally show respect to your father? Are you currently withholding respect from your husband? Would you be willing to try this out for a week by genuinely complimenting your undeserving husband and see if it makes a difference?

A great way to wash one's wife's feet is through positive behaviours. Marriage researcher Dr. John Gottman has found that successful marriages have, on average, five times more encouraging, positive behaviours than negative behaviours.[312] Encouraging behaviours can consist of doing simple things. A healthy marriage celebrates the ordinary, not just the extraordinary. Janice and Ed are learning afresh the joy of ordinary pleasures: taking regular time together for peaceful walks, chatting over a cup of tea, listening to each other's daily experiences, watching a video together, going out for dinner, and even reading together. Ed and Janice often read side by side on the couch or in bed. Ed loves hearing Janice read the Bible out loud. We also enjoy working out at the gym, going for a swim, and visiting close relatives or friends. Spending time with the one you love doesn't have to cost a lot of money, but the payoff is priceless. When you spend special time together, enjoying each other's company, it's far easier to forgive each other when those difficult situations inevitably come up. Foot washing and making up go well together, for better, for worse.

Husbands, according to Ephesians 5:26–27, are called to daily wash their wife with the water of God's Word, making her radiant, without stain, wrinkle, or any other blemish. The mutuality of our marriage covenant calls husbands to share in making our wives holy and blameless, whole and self-differentiated. Many women live with generational blame and shame. Husbands can be used to help their wives live in blamelessness, no longer self-condemning. Many women can be very hard on themselves, self-accusing as not being a good enough mother, a good enough spouse, a good enough daughter. The husband is called to remove his wife's many wrinkles, just as Christ removes His bride's many wrinkles. Bruce insightfully commented, "The Church as it is seen in our actual experience at the present time falls far short of this ideal; spots and wrinkles are abundantly in evidence."[313]

Many highly attractive women secretly feel ugly. Ed spontaneously speaks of Janice's beauty every day. Janice is not only physically beautiful to Ed. He is drawn to the beauty of her inner spirit, what the Good Book calls the unfading beauty of an gentle and quiet spirit, which is of great worth in God's sight.[314] Part of Janice's attractiveness to Ed is because she is clothed with strength and dignity. Likewise, Jesus is drawn to the beauty of His bride for whom He shed his blood. He doesn't see us as an ugly duckling. We may feel like Cinderella, but Jesus sees us as a beautiful princess dressed in wedding clothes.[315] We are told in Ephesians 5:29 how Christ feeds and cares for His bride. Husbands similarly need to care for their wives, to love and cherish them, till death do them part. The most self-differentiated husbands are the most caring, for better, for worse. Wounded wives often feel uncared for and not listened to. They often say, "If my husband really loved me, he would change." The Greek word *thalpei,* translated here as *care* or *cherish,* is used elsewhere once only in 1 Thessalonians 2:12 to describe a mother gently nursing her children. The Bible commentator, Williamson, says that *thalpei* (care) means to warm. Christ not only cherishes and cares about us but He understands us better than anyone else ever will. He is the foundation upon which Janice and Ed have built their marriage, and the reason they are even more in love forty years later.

Ed's dream is that husbands could grow as gentle men in the gentleness of Jesus as they warmly cherish and nourish their wives. Would you, as husbands, be willing to commit to nurturing your wife through taking her on a date once a week? Would you be willing to cherish your wife through giving her an hour a day of your undivided attention, actively listening to her as she shares her heart with you? Too often husbands fall very short of the covenantal ideal for marriage, too frequently being left with regrets, broken dreams, and marital cutoff. Lord, have covenant mercy on us and our marriages.

The marriage wisdom of Ephesians 5 is explicitly rooted in the marriage covenant in Genesis Chapter 2. Both Jesus (in Mark 10:7) and Paul quoted Genesis 2:24 in which male/female monogamy is affirmed as God's created order and intention for marriage. Whenever polygamy occurred in the Old Testament, it was consistently linked with marital difficulty. Never in the New Testament was a husband called to lay his life down for his harem. The bride in Ephesians 5 is distinctly singular, as is Jesus' singular bride, the Church. Jesus is spiritually monogamous. Without Jesus' and Paul's reaffirming the monogamous trajectory of Genesis 2:24, it is quite possible that, as with Islam and early Mormonism, polygamy might have been widespread and even normative in Christianity. Wherever Christianity makes a significant impact around the world, monogamy seems to become the cultural default. For how many generations has your family of origin been monogamous? In some parts of the world, Christians are the first or second generation to have embraced the gift of monogamy. Gender equality and monogamy are closely related biblical gifts.

We in North America have largely lost a sense of the covenantal mystery of what it means both to be married and to be Christ's bridal Church. After speaking in Ephesians 5:31 about Genesis 2:24, Paul calls covenant marriage "a great or profound mystery." The Latin Vulgate Bible translated the Greek term *mysterion* as *sacrament.* The Eastern Church still calls the sacraments *mysteries.*[316] Many Protestant commentators have rejected the concept of marriage as a sacrament, preferring to call it an *ordinance.* The term *ordinance* is somewhat sterile, and therefore we prefer the terms *covenant, sacrament,* or even *mystery.* Either way marriage is, as Paul said, a great mystery. How is your spouse a mystery to you, for better, for worse?

Janice sometimes thinks that she has Ed all figured out. Then suddenly he will tell her a story about his childhood that she never heard before. Just when Ed thinks he knows the next step, Janice will surprise with an important new idea that stretches their thinking and situation.

Christ's covenantal relation to his bride, the Church, is mysteriously paralleled to the husband's covenantal relation to his bride. The "one flesh" covenant relationship of husband and wife, for Paul, foreshadows and demonstrates the covenant relationship between Christ and the Church. Paul goes back and forth almost seamlessly in Ephesians 5, discussing both parallel covenants.[317] Jesus was clear in Mark 12:25 that our male/female marriage covenant is temporary for this life only, but the marriage covenant between Christ and his people is eternal. The first covenant is temporary, the second ultimate. We see this as all the more reason to not take our marital disagreements too seriously and to value our earthly marriage in the short time that we have together as husband and wife.

Ed was initially reluctant to believe that the marriage covenant was temporary for this life only. He was so emotionally fused to Janice that he could not imagine eternity without being married to her. Over time, Ed has realized that only his covenant relationship with Jesus is permanent. By putting Janice on the altar, Ed has learned how to emotionally hold Janice more lightly with open arms. Letting go and letting God is at the heart of self-differentiation. Do you need to let go and hold your spouse more lightly, for better, for worse, till death do you part?

Because Christ's bride, the Church, is going to outlast our own earthly marriage, it is vital for each of us to be connected to a healthy local church. Marriages suffer when we isolate ourselves from others. We were never meant to do marriage alone. Shared spirituality and community help protect our marriages while simultaneously helping to satisfy our individual needs to feel understood. Gathering with other believers and building relationships within a community of brothers and sisters in Christ can be a huge source of strength. Ordinary practices such as attending church, reading the Bible, and praying together have been scientifically shown to strengthen marriages.[318] Are you currently emotionally cut off or disconnected from a loving church family? Would you be willing to try out a local church for three months and see if it helps strengthen your marriage?

Praying together softens each one's heart toward the other. Even if your spouse doesn't want to pray with you, your prayers will still have an effect. Prayer has an amazing ability to change our stubbornness into openness. Have you ever wondered what the Holy Spirit wants to say to both of you about your marriage? Prayer can radically transform a marriage when couples start listening for the still small voice of God. In many marriages struggling with problems with finances, in-laws, and children, Janice and Ed have seen helpful changes after couples started to pray together. It's best to start simply, perhaps repeating the Lord's Prayer together, and then gradually learn to pray more spontaneously, remembering that the essence of prayer is learning to say to God thank you, sorry, and please. Sadly, we've found that many couples view the idea of praying together as too intimate; one or both spouses may feel awkward about showing emotion or vulnerability. Prayer, for many, is more intimate than sex. They may have never seen their parents pray together in public. If our relationship with God is the most important thing in our lives, then sharing that relationship by praying aloud to our Heavenly Father reinforces our bond as a couple. Jointly thanking God for the many good things in our lives and seeking His wisdom for the problems we face, makes us closer to each other and to the Lord. Prayer can even help our covenantal differentiation in marriage, for better, for worse. Would you be willing to experiment for a week in praying with your spouse? Start simple.

Covenantal Differentiation in Marriage

The more differentiated a spouse is, the healthier and holier will be the covenantal marriage. Covenantal differentiation strengthens marriages and bridges cutoff. Richardson suggests that becoming a more differentiated self might be included in our concept of sanctification.[319] The term *sanctification* refers to holiness, wholeness, and Christ-likeness, all helpful features in a healthy marriage. In self-differentiation, we echo Martin Luther's statement "Here I stand."[320] Taking principled stands in one's marriage is essential to being one's true self, for better, for worse. Prior to his death in 1990, Bowen was working on his ninth concept: spirituality.[321] He called it "the Supernatural." Bowen was attempting to find an objective way to speak about the subjective areas of our beliefs and how they impact our behaviours. He did not continue his work, he said, because of the intense emotional reactivity of the profession to it. Gilbert wonders if he left that developmental work for others of this and future generations.[322]

Nichols comments that throughout the 20th century, psychotherapists tried to keep religion out of the counselling session. As a result, they never asked people about meaning and spirituality.[323] Some of a family's most powerful organizing beliefs have to do with how they find meaning in their lives and their ideas about a higher power. The clearer our life principles, the more we can live out our Christian faith in a differentiated way. The responsible self is the faithful self, full of faith and alignment with one's core values.[324] By patterning our lives after Jesus, we are modelling our lives on that of a very highly self-differentiated individual. To call Jesus highly self-differentiated expresses the fullness of his humanity but does not sum up the fullness of his divinity. Christ-centredness and Christ-likeness are at the heart of the Christian covenant of marriage. Bowen himself said that Christians should pattern their lives after that of Jesus.[325] The way of marital wisdom involves the ability to think for oneself, like Christ did, rather than anxiously collapse into reactive groupthink. Would you like to thoughtfully explore the way of Jesus as a key to strengthening your covenant marriage?

A strong motivator for Ed doing his doctorate thesis on strengthening marriages was a time of renewal with Elias Antonas in 1996 on the North Shore of Vancouver, where we met six nights a week for three months. During that time, we saw the restoration of many marriages that looked like they were over. Through a powerful encounter with Christ, many people self-differentiated from their emotional fusion to their spouses and worked instead on their own personal issues. Again and again we saw marital cutoff bridged in apparently hopeless situations. One former North Shore couple, both of whom are lawyers, have sent Ed a basket of fruit every Christmas as a way of expressing their gratitude for the marriage strengthening they received during that season of renewal. The restoration of marriages and bridging cutoff has become an unshakable calling for us.

An Amazing Love Story

What might it be like to be married to a very strong and famous world-traveller? The late Billy Graham, who died at age 99, was named for the sixtieth consecutive year in a Gallup poll as one of the ten most admired people in the world, along with Pope Francis and Bill Gates.[326] It was Ruth Graham, his devoted, differentiated wife for sixty-three years, who enabled Billy Graham to be healthy in the midst of relentless international attention. Without Ruth's loving care for their five children, it would have been impossible for Billy Graham to have taken part in 417 city-wide celebrations in 185 countries, speaking to live audiences of nearly 215 million people.[327] Billy and Ruth Graham were a covenant love story that we can all learn from, for better, for worse.

Ruth, who lived her first seventeen years in China, never wanted to marry, intending instead to become a missionary in Tibet. After going to school in North Korea, she moved to Wheaton College in Illinois. There, in 1940, she met Billy, who instantly fell in love with her. Ruth was slightly startled by his intense blue eyes. As her biographer, Patricia Cornwell, put it, "Billy was unlike anyone Ruth had met ... earnest, quietly confident, and personal. Clearly, he spoke as one who knew God and knew him well.... But what interested Ruth was that as Billy escorted her..., he seemed completely unaware of his uniqueness, his poignancy, his gift."[328] Billy was very nervous around Ruth but eventually invited Ruth to hear Handel's *Messiah* with him. That night Ruth knelt on the carpet by her bed and prayed, "God, if You let me serve with that man, I'd consider it the greatest privilege in my life."[329]

Ruth wrote to her medical missionary parents in China, saying, "Despite Bill's fearlessness and sometimes sternness, he is just as thoughtful and gentle as you want a man to be.... [H]e makes you feel perfectly natural and looked after without being showy or obnoxious. Sounds like I'm in love, doesn't it? Don't get worried. I'm not."[330] Both Billy and Ruth were independent and very determined people, which led to some early challenges in their relationship. It was normal in Ruth's family for women to be strong and outspoken, something that Billy had to get used to. In writing to her parents in 1941, she said, "[Billy] isn't easy to love because of his sternness and unwavering stand on certain issues. Many a night I have come in almost hating the man because I wanted my way in some little thing that was either unwise or foolish or something, and he wouldn't give in even if it meant losing my love."[331] Sometimes Billy and Ruth could be the immovable object and the irresistible force. Writing to her parents later in 1941, she said, "[Billy] has his faults and some people object to his fearless, uncompromising presentation of the gospel. But that was the first thing about him that commanded my attention and later my admiration—as I grew to know him better, my trust."[332]

After accepting his marriage proposal, she visited her sister Rosa in a New Mexico TB sanatorium. While visiting there, she herself suffered from exhaustion. In that condition, she wrote Billy a crushing letter, telling him that she didn't think that she was in love with him and that marriage was perhaps unwise.[333] Her sister miraculously recovered, and Ruth went ahead with the wedding. Cornwell commented, "What Ruth would do next, no one could predict, for she was as quietly stubborn as the sphinx and just about as inscrutable.... She didn't necessarily do the practical or the expected."[334]

One of the greatest challenges to their marriage was how much Billy was away. Ruth often said, "I would rather have a little of Bill than a lot of any other man."[335] Many of Billy Graham's sermon illustrations came directly from Ruth's voracious reading of biographies, histories, novels, and books about art and foreign countries. It was Ruth's deep faith in God that kept her going through many trying times. She taught that a happy marriage is the union of two good forgivers. One time, after Billy unexpectedly went with his buddies to Chicago without Ruth, she tearfully prayed, "God, if you forgive me for marrying him, I'll never do it again." When he realized how much he had hurt her, he was full of tender apologies.[336] Ruth often said, "Sometimes beautiful women develop from adjusting to difficult men."[337] By all accounts, Ruth was a beautiful woman in body, mind, and spirit. Her medical missionary dad, her evangelist husband Billy, and her beloved prodigal son Franklin, all helped her become more beautiful and self-differentiated.

In 1963, Billy romantically wrote to Ruth:

> How can I find words to express my appreciation for all you have meant to me? Your love and patience with me in my ups and downs … have meant more to me than you will ever know. Your counsel, advice, encouragement, and prayer have been my mainstay…. It seems in the recent months my capacity to love you has deepened…. I love the wife of my youth more every day! Yes, I am thankful to God for you…. No child ever had a greater mother than our children.[338]

Ruth and Billy lived out the four key marriage principles of rediscovering strengths, celebrating differences, valuing conflict, and balancing closeness and personal space. They loved and cherished each other, for better or worse, till death did them part.

"For better, for worse" is a covenant promise. Are you willing, like Billy and Ruth, to make that promise today, perhaps for the first time? God the covenant maker calls us to covenant-keeping in our marriages. Covenantal differentiation reduces cutoff and strengthens marriages. God's yes in the covenantal sacrament of marriage is "Yes and Amen," a clear divine yes in a cutoff world. Will you join us in saying yes to God's gift of covenant marriage, both in your life and for the sake of other marriages? Are you willing to say "I do"?

Glossary of Terms used in Family Systems Theory

Anxiety: It is the fear of a real or imagined threat that brings heightened reactivity. It is a physiological arousal preparatory to action to preserve the safety of the individual. Anxiety can be acute and short term or chronic and long term, even crossing the generations in a family system. As the most contagious emotion, it is the crucial issue.

Basic self: The core self is rooted in guiding principles, goals, vision, and values. It is the inner guidance system, the "person of the person." This contrasts with the pseudo or functional self, which gives away self, lacks healthy boundaries, and is emotionally fused to others.

Boundaries: They are delineations between people and between systems. Boundaries, when clear and flexible, are an expression of self-differentiation, permitting people to be close without emotional fusion. Rigid boundaries are an expression of anxiety and unresolved emotional attachment.

Bowen Theory (or Family Systems Theory): It is a theory developed by Murray Bowen that involved eight interlocking concepts for understanding systemic biological patterns. It is inherently multigenerational, seeing the present as rooted in past family relationships, in one's family of origin. Bowen Theory involves systemic thinking in contrast to a linear cause-and-effect approach. It sees the family as an emotional unit, a network of interlocking relationships.

Cutoff (or emotional cutoff): Bowen defined his last Family Systems Theory concept, "emotional cutoff," as the process of separation, isolation, withdrawal, running away, or denying the importance of the parental family. It primarily describes how people disconnect from their past in order to begin their lives in the current generation. Emotional cutoff is the extreme form of unresolved emotional distance. As an expression of closeness anxiety, it is the polar opposite of emotional fusion. Cutoffs are either primary—when directly related to one's parents—or secondary, indirect, and inherited—when based on interlocking triangles and on the multigenerational emotional process, which can be traced back to the primary parental cutoff by the person. In light of Bowen's use of the phrase "separation of people from each other" to describe cutoff, the term *cutoff* can be applied to other relationships than just the parent–child relationship.

Detriangulation: It is the process of emotional detaching from family triangles, while remaining calmly present, so as not to be emotionally fused with other members of a triangle.

Differentiation (or differentiation of self, self-differentiation, or individuation): It is the foundation and cornerstone concept of Family Systems Theory. Differentiation involves distinguishing between the thinking, feeling, and emotional systems. Bowen saw differentiation as equivalent to identity and individuality.

It is the use of the cognitive, the neocortex, to control the instinctual, the amygdala. As the antidote to emotional cutoff, differentiation is a lifelong process rather than a completed state.

Emotion: Bowen used the term *emotion* as synonymous with instinct rather than with feelings. Instinct is seen biologically rather than psychoanalytically. He acknowledged that this was a minority position. Such automatic responses involved the fight, flight, or freeze reactions are connected to the amygdala part of the brain.

Emotional fusion: It involves a loss of self and a lack of boundaries in relationships. Emotion and reason merge in a way that reduces thoughtfulness and choice. Togetherness swallows individuality and increases anxiety.

Family emotional processes (or nuclear family emotional processes): They are multigenerational emotional patterns such as 1) emotional distance, 2) symptoms in one's spouse or family, 3) significant marital and/or family conflict, and 4) projection of anxiety onto one's children.

Family of origin: It is the family into which a person was born or adopted. Work on one's family of origin is key to a breakthrough in self-differentiation, even more so than with personal counselling. The use of a genogram is invaluable in family-of-origin exploration.

Family projection process: It is the projection of anxiety and conflict onto other family members, particularly in a multigenerational manner. Such projection reduces the ability of the child to self-differentiate and to relate to one's future spouse and family. Such a pattern is closely involved with blaming and scapegoating others as the IP– (identified person negative).

Genogram: It is a multigenerational map that one draws to more objectively show the emotional processes and patterns of one's family, including emotional cutoff, distance, conflict, emotional fusion, and triangling.

Homeostasis: It is the polarized rejection of change and the mandating of "business as usual" in an emotional family system. Sameness and apparent security are reactively chosen over transformation and the embracing of a thoughtful new future. This fear of upsetting systemic equilibrium brings a loss of flexibility, curiosity, and growth. Homeostatic "stuckness" is usually multigenerational in nature and impact, resulting in both emotional fusion and cutoff.

Identified person (IP): In family emotional systems and triangles, there is often a person who is initially pedestalized and treated as the IP positive rescuer. Another person, perhaps the same person in another relationship phase, will be treated as the IP negative, the outsider, the scapegoat and the alleged cause of the family anxiety. Having identified people is a common way to avoid dealing with our own anxiety and unwillingness to change.

Marital conflict: It is a patterned way of reacting to anxious emotional fusion. Projection of blame is common. Chronic marital conflict is that which lasts two years or longer on one or numerous issues. Bowen describes marital conflict as involving an intense amount of emotional energy in which neither spouse gives in to the other on major issues.[339] Conflict can bring greater marital intimacy and self-differentiation when differences are embraced and appreciated.

Multigenerational transmission process: This is the focus of Family Systems Theory coaching, rather than concentrating on presenting issues. Becoming more aware of one's family-of-origin patterns allows people to objectively learn about where they have come from generationally and where they are potentially heading.

Overfunctioning: It is doing too much in a way that brings emotional fusion with others, loss of self, and a reduction of others' functioning. Overfunctioning involves an unhealthy overresponsibility for and rescuing of others.

Pseudo-self (or functional self): It is the pretend self that is highly shaped by other's expectation and by anxious reactivity. During times of stress, it either disappears into fused togetherness or becomes rigidly reactive. The pseudo-self is the imitation of the core or solid self.

Reactivity: It is the homeostatic emotional patterns that develop when anxiety and conflict are high. Reactivity, in contrast to responsiveness, expresses the instinctive nature of the amygdala and lacks the thoughtful contribution of the neocortex. The lower the self-differentiation, the higher the reactivity. When people become upset, they may reactively yell, blame, or go to silence and cutoff.

Responsiveness: It is the thoughtful interaction with other members of a family or family system. Responsiveness involves the power of choice rather than just instinctively reacting. It is heightened by family-of-origin work and self-differentiation.

System (or emotional system): It is the network of interconnected relationships. Such emotional units may include marriages, families, church, community groups, etc. Bowen taught that any relationship with balancing forces and counter forces in constant operation is a system. Richardson describes a system as like a hanging mobile with interconnected pieces.

Triangle: Triangles, as the smallest stable emotional unit, are the universal unit of analysis. Anxiety causes the marriage dyad to bring in a third person, be it a child, friend, relative, or counsellor. Triangles, a fact of nature, describe the what, how, when, and where of marriage relationships, not the why. Most triangles unhelpfully treat one member of the triangle as an outsider or as the IP negative/scapegoat.

Triangulation: It is the playing of the child by one parent against the other parent during conflict. Such behaviour produces calmness by projecting the marital anxiety onto the child. Triangulation is an effective way to avoid working on one's own self-differentiation.

Unresolved emotional attachment: This is defined by Titelman as the emotional degree to which a person is unable to move forward in the process toward increasing independence, unable to be a self and define a self in relationship to important others. It defines the relationship between emotional and intellectual functioning, bringing a rigid, dependent fusion dominated by the automatic emotional system.

BIBLIOGRAPHY

Adorney, Abby P., *The Relationship of Emotional Cutoff to Marital Function and Psychological Symptom Development*, PhD in Psychology Dissertation (California School of Professional Psychology, Los Angeles, 1993).

Akers-Woody, Michele Denise, *Understanding the Attitudes Toward Marriage of Never-Married Female Young Adult Children of Divorce using Bowen Theory*, PsyD Dissertation (Alliant International University, San Diego, ProQuest Dissertations and Theses, 2003).

Anonymous (thought to be Bowen), "Toward the Differentiation of a Self in one's own Family" (Sydney, AU: The Family Systems Institute, 1972).

Anderson, H., D. Browning, E. Evison, and M. Van Leeuwen, *The Family Book* (Louisville, KY: Westminster John Knox Press, 1998).

Anderson, Ray, and Dennis Guernsey, *On Being Family: A Social Theology of the Family* (Grand Rapids, MI: Eerdmans, 1985).

Arnold, Richard L., *Practical Application of a Theologically Integrated, Systemic Theory for Marriage and Family Therapy*, DMin thesis (Gordon-Conwell Theological Seminary, June 2003).

Balswick, Jack and Judith, *The Family: A Christian perspective on the contemporary home* (Grand Rapids, MI: Baker Book House, 1989).

Balswick, Jack and Judith, *A Model for Marriage: Covenant, Grace, Empowerment and Intimacy* (Downers Grove, IL: IVP Academic, 2006).

Baly, Denis, *God and History in the Old Testament* (New York, NY: Harper and Row Publishers, 1976).

Barth, Markus, *Ephesians 4–6: The anchor Bible* (Garden City, NY: Double Day & Company Inc., 1974).

Baughen, Michael and Myrtle, *Christian Marriage: A handbook for couples* (Grand Rapids, MI: Baker Books, 1994).

Becvar, Dorothy Stroh, and Ralph J. Becvar, *Family Therapy: A systemic integration*, 2nd Edition (Boston: St. Louis Family Institute, Allyn and Bacon, 1993, 1998).

Benson, Kyle, "The Magic Art of Relationships According to Science," October 4, 2017. https://www.gottman.com/blog/the-magic-relationshIP–ratio-according-science/ (Accessed Oct. 17, 2017).

Biography.com, Billy Graham Biography, http://www.biography.com/people/billy-graham-9317669 (Accessed October 29, 2017).

The Book of Common Prayer, (Toronto: Anglican Book Centre, 1962).

Bowen, Murray, "Family Systems Theory," in Philip J. Guerin (Ed.), *Family Therapy: Theory and Practice*, (New York: Gardner Press, 1976). Also published in Murray Bowen, *Family Therapy in Clinical Practice* (New York: Aronson, 1978).

Bowen, Murray, *Family Therapy in Clinical Practice* (New York, NY: Jason Aaronson Inc.,1985, 1983, 1978, 1992)

Bowen, Murray, *The Origins of Family Psychotherapy: The NIMH Family Study Project*, (J. Butler, ed.) (Lanham, MD: Jason Aronson, 2013).

Bowen, Murray, "Theory in the Practice of Psychotherapy," in P. J. Guerin (Ed.). *Family Therapy: Theory and Practice* (New York, NY: Gardner Press, 1976).

Bowen, Murray, "The Use of Family Theory in Clinical Practice," *Comprehensive Psychiatry* 7:345–374, 1966.

Bowen, Murray, "Various Theoretical Points People Miss: A training session by Dr. Murray Bowen at the Minnesota Institute of Family Dynamics," in O.C. Bregman and C. M. White (Eds.), *Bringing Systems Thinking to Life* (New York, NY: Routledge Taylor & Francis Group, 2011).

Bowlby, John, *Attachment and Loss: Vol. 1, 2, and 3* (London, UK: Penguin Books, 1969, 1973, 1980).

Bregman, Ona Cohn, "Preface," in O.C Bregman and C. M. White (Eds.), *Bringing Systems Thinking to Life: Expanding the horizons for Bowen Family Systems Theory*, (New York, NY: Routledge Taylor & Francis Group, 2011).

Bromiley, G.W., *Baptism and the Anglican Reformers* (London, UK: Lutherworth Press, 1953).

Browning, Robert, "Rabbi Ben Ezra," https://www.poetryfoundation.org/poems/43775/rabbi-ben-ezra (Accessed October 17, 2017).

Bruce, F.F., *The Epistle to the Ephesians* (London, UK: Pickering & Inglis Ltd, 1961).

Canon, George E., *The Use of Traditional Material in Colossians* (Macon, GA: Mercer University Press, 1983).

Joseph C. Carolin (Ed.), *Marriage and Family Therapy: Psychoanalytic, Behavioral and systems theory perspectives: Systems and spirituality: Bowen Systems Theory, faith and theology,* the papers and proceedings of a conference on theology held at Washington Theological Union (Washington, DC: July 1987).

Cartredge, Mark J., and David Mills, *Covenant Theology: Contemporary Approaches* (Carlisle, UK: Paternoster Press, 2001).

Coles, John and Anne, *Making More of Marriage* (Berkhamsted, UK: New Wine International Publishing, 2000).

Cornwell, Patricia Daniels, *A Time for Remembering: The Ruth Bell Graham story* (San Francisco: Harper & Row, 1983).

Crabb, Larry, *Men and Women: Enjoying the difference* (Grand Rapids, MI: Zondervan Publishing House, 1991).

Davids, Peter and Judy, "Healing the Bleeding Wound: Divorce and remarriage: Biblical teaching, pastoral strategies, healing approaches" (Houston, TX: PJD Ministries, 2009), http://www.davidsnet.ws/biblical.

Dillard, C.K., and H.O. Protinsky, "Emotional Cutoff: A comparative analysis of clinical versus non-clinical populations," *International Journal of Family Psychiatry*, 6, 1985.

Dinkmeyer, Don, and Jon Carlson, *Time for a Better Marriage* (Circle Pines, MN: American Guidance Service, 1984).

Ducklow, Paddy, "Appreciative Inquiry: A paradigm shift for social systems," http://theducklows.ca/downloads/AISystemsChange.pdf.

Ducklow, Paddy, "Anxiety is the transmitter of generational pain," Carey Theological College, October 18, 2012.

Ducklow, Paddy, *Coaching Church Leaders in Conflict: Resolving strategies using family systems theory,* doctoral thesis (Deerfield, IL: Trinity International University, December 2002).

Ducklow, Paddy, Conflicted Church/Conflicted Leader course, Carey Theological College, Fall 2011.

Ducklow, Paddy, Principle #7: Ministry Is Risking Failure, https://www.vista.ubc.ca/webct/RelativeResourceManager/Template/Manual%202011%20Appendices.pdf.

Dumbrell, William J., *Covenant and Creation: An Old Testament covenantal theology* (Exeter, UK: Paternoster Press, 1984).

Dunn, James G., *Epistles to Colossians and Philemon* (Grand Rapids, MI: Eerdmans Publishing, 1996).

Epimenides, *Cretica*, Prof. J. Rendel Harris (Trans.), the *Expositor* (Oct. 1906, 305–17; Apr. 1907, 332–37; Apr. 1912, 348–353).

Espinosa, Eddie, "Change My Heart, Oh God," (Vineyard Music, 1995) https://www.youtube.com/watch?v=DwudqCO7mSQ (Accessed October 24, 2017).

Fetch, Shan, and Dawn Macomb, "Generational Healing: A client's experience of an intervention to promote forgiveness and healing the generational bond," *Marriage and Family: A Christian Journal,* Vol. 4, Issue 2, 2001.

Framo, James L., "Family of Origin as a Therapeutic Resource for Adults and Marital and Family Therapy: You can and should go home again," *Family Process*, 15:193–210, 1976.

Freeman, David S., *Family Therapy with Couples: The family-of-origin approach* (New Jersey: Jason Aronson Inc., 1992).

Freeman, David S., "A Model for Teaching a Beginner's Course on Family Therapy," in *Family Practice* (UBC School of Social Work).

Friedman, Edwin, *Body and Soul in Family Process*, video (the Pastoral Care Association of BC 4th Annual Conference, 1991).

Friedman, Edwin, *Bowen Theory and Therapy,* (PsycINFO Database Record (c) 2012 APA), p. 149. https://www.researchgate.net/publication/232485321_Bowen_theory_and_therapy (Accessed January 23, 2018).

Friedman, Edwin, *A Failure of Nerve: Leadership in an age of the quick-fix* (Bethesda, MD: The Edwin Friedman Estate/Trust, 1999).

Friedman, Edwin, *Generation to Generation* (New York, NY: The Guilford Press, 1985).

Friesen, Priscilla J., "Emotional Cutoff and the Brain" in Peter Titelman (Ed.), *Emotional Cutoff: Bowen Family Systems Theory perspective* (New York, NY: The Haworth Clinical Practice Press, 2003).

Frost, Randall T., "Thinking Systems in Pastoral Training," in Bregman and White (Eds.) *Bringing Systems Thinking to Life: Expanding the horizons for Bowen family systems theory,* (New York, NY: Routledge, 2010).

Fulwiler, Michael, "Managing Conflict: Solvable Versus Perpetual Problems," The Gottman Relationship Blog, https://www.gottman.com/blog/managing-conflict-solvable-vs-perpetual-problems/.

Garland, Diana R., *Family Ministry: A Comprehensive Guide* (Downers Grove, IL: IVP Academic, 1999).

Gilbert, Roberta, *The Cornerstone Concept: In leadership, in life* (Virginia: Leading Systems Press, 2008).

Gilbert, Roberta M., *The Eight Concepts of Bowen Theory: A new way of thinking about the individual and the group* (Virginia: Leading Systems Press, 2004, 2006).

Gilbert, Roberta, *Extraordinary Leadership: Thinking systems, making a difference* (Virginia: Leading Systems Press, 2006).

Gilbert, Roberta, *Extraordinary Relationships: A new way of thinking about human interactions* (Minneapolis, MN: Chronimed Publishing, 1992).

Gotlieb, Eileen, "Emotional Cutoff and Holocaust Survivors," in Peter Titelman (Ed.), *Emotional Cutoff: Bowen Family Systems Theory perspective* (New York, NY: The Haworth Clinical Practice Press, 2003).

Grabe, Petrus J., *New Covenant, New Community: The significance of biblical and patristic covenant theology for current understanding* (Bletchley, UK: Paternoster Press, 2006).

Grant, Jamie A., and Alistair I. Wilson, *The God of Covenant: Biblical, theological and contemporary perspectives* (Leicester, UK: Apollos, IVP, 2005).

Hahn, Scott, *Covenant and Communion* (Grand Rapids, MI: Brazos Press, Baker Publishing Group, 2009).

Hahn, Scott, *First Comes Love: Finding your family in the church and the trinity* (New York, NY: Doubleday, 2002).

Harley, William Jr., *His Needs, Her Needs* (Old Tappan, NJ: Fleming H. Revell Company, 1986).

Harris, Murray J., *Colossians and Philemon: Exegetical guide to the New Testament* (Grand Rapids, MI: Eerdmans Publishing, 1991).

Harrison, Everett F., *Colossians: Christ All-Sufficient* (Chicago, IL: Moody Press, 1971).

Haverluck, Michael F., "Sweet 60: Billy Graham one of 10 'Most Admired Men' again," One News Now, January 8, 2017, https://www.onenewsnow.com/culture/2017/01/08/sweet-60-billy-graham-one-of-10-most-admired-men-again (Accessed October 29, 2017).

Hawkins, Yasmin, Jane Ussher, Emilee Gilbert, Janette Perz, Mirjana Sandoval, and Kendra Sundquist, "Changes in Sexuality and Intimacy After the Diagnosis and Treatment of Cancer: The Experience of Partners in a Sexual Relationship With a Person With Cancer" (*Cancer Nursing*, Vol. 32, No. 4, 2009).

Hay, David M., *Colossians* (Nashville, TN: Abingdon Press, 2000).

Hendrix, Harville, *Getting the Love You Want: A guide for couples* (New York, NY: Harper & Row Publishers, 1988).

Hird, Ed, "Rationale for the Wedding Service" (Vancouver, BC: Vancouver School of Theology, 1977).

Hird, Ed and Janice, Strengthening Marriage Workshop, transcript, available on request.

Hoehner, Harold W., *Ephesians Cornerstone Biblical Commentary* (Carol Stream, IL: Tyndale, 2008).

Horton, Michael, *God of Promise: Introducing covenant theology* (Grand Rapids, MI: Baker Books, 2006).

Horton, Michael, *Putting Amazing Back into Grace* (Nashville, TN: Thomas Nelson Publisher, 2001).

Horton, Michael S., *Covenant and Eschatology: The divine drama* (Louisville, KY: Westminster John Knox Press, 2002).

Horton, Michael S., *Covenant and Salvation: Union with Christ* (Louisville, KY: Westminster John Knox Press, 2007).

Horton, Michael S., *Lord and Servant: A covenant Christology* (Louisville, KY: Westminster John Knox Press, 2005).

Horton, Michael S., *People and Place: A covenant ecclesiology* (Louisville, KY: Westminster John Knox Press, 2008).

Howe, Leroy T. "Self-Differentiation in Christian Perspective," *Pastoral Psychology*, Vol. 46, No. 5, 1998, p. 349.

Hugenberger, Gordon P., *Marriage as a Covenant: Biblical law and ethics as developed from Malachi* (Grand Rapids, MI: Baker Books, 1994).

Hunt, Richard and Joan, *Awaken Your Power to Love* (Nashville, TN: Thomas Nelson Publishers, 1994).

Illick, Selden Dunbar, et al., "Toward Understanding and Measuring Emotional Cutoff," in Peter Titelman (Ed.), *Emotional Cutoff: Bowen Family Systems Theory perspective* (New York, NY: The Haworth Clinical Practice Press, 2003).

Imber-Black, Evan, *Secrets in Families and Family Therapy* (New York, NY: Norton, 1993).

Instone-Brewer, David, *Divorce and Remarriage in the Church: Biblical solutions for pastoral realities* (Bletchley, UK: Paternoster Press, 2003).

Jacobsen, Neil S., and Alan S. Gurnman (Eds.), *Clinical Handbook of Couple Therapy* (New York, NY: Guilford Press, 1995).

James, Muriel, *Marriage is for Loving* (Reading, MA: Addison-Wesley Publishing Company, 1979).

Jones, E. Stanley, *Victory Through Surrender* (Nashville, TN: Abingdon Publications, 1980).

Jones, Susan L., *Family Therapy: A comparison of approaches* (Bowie, MD: Robert Brady Co., 1980).

Karpel, Mark A., "Family Secrets: Conceptual and ethical issues in the relational context," in *Family Process,* 1980 (19), pp. 295–306.

Keller, Tim and Kathy, *The Meaning of Marriage* (New York, NY: Dutton, Penguin Group, 2012).

Kendall, R.T., *Calvin and English Calvinism to 1649* (Oxford, UK: Oxford University Press, 1979).

Kerr, Michael E., "Chronic Anxiety and Defining a Self," *The Atlantic Monthly*, Sept. 1988.

Kerr, Michael E., "Family Systems Theory and Therapy," in *Handbook of family therapy*, Gurman and Kniskern (Eds.) (New York, NY: Routledge, 1981).

Kerr, Michael E., and Murray Bowen, *Family Evaluation: An approach based on Bowen Theory* (W.W. Norton & Company, 1988).

Klever, "Marital Functioning and Multigenerational Fusion and Cutoff," in Peter Titelman (Ed.), *Emotional Cutoff: Bowen Family Systems Theory perspective* (New York, NY: The Haworth Clinical Practice Press, 2003).

Kline, Meredith G., *The Structure of Biblical Authority* (Grand Rapids, MI: Baker Books, 1975).

Konstam, Angus, *The History of Pirates* (New York, NY: The Lyons Press, 1999).

Leach, William H. (Ed.), *The Cokesbury Marriage Manual* (Nashville, TN: Abingdon Pres, 1939, 1961).

Lederer, William J., *Creating a Good Relationship* (New York, NY: WW Norton & Company, 1981, 1984).

Lee, Nicky and Sila, *The Marriage Course: How to build a lasting relationship,* Leader's Guide and Manual, (London, UK: HTB Publications, 2000).

Lillback, Peter A., *The Binding of God: Calvin's role in the development of covenant theology* (Grand Rapids, MI: Baker Academics, 2001).

Lisitsa, Ellie, "The Four Horsemen," https://www.gottman.com/blog/category/column/the-four-horsemen (Accessed Oct. 20, 2017).

Lohse, Eduard, *Colossians and Philemon* (Philadelphia, PA: Fortress Press, 1971, 1975).

Mace, David and Vera, *We Can Have Better Marriages if We Really Want Them* (Nashville, TN: Abingdon, 1974, 1978).

MacLean, Paul D., *A Triune Concept of the Brain and Behaviour* (Toronto, ON: University of Toronto Press, 1973).

Martin, Christopher Scott, *Getting the Picture: Composing a family portrait through cognitive-behavioral and family systems therapy*, DMin Thesis (Gordon-Conwell Theological Seminary, Feb. 27, 2004).

McManus, Michael J., *Marriage Savers: Helping Your Friends and Family Stay Married* (Grand Rapids, MI: Zondervan Publishing House, 1993).

McNeal, Reggie, *A Work of Heart: Understanding how God shapes spiritual leaders* (New York, NY: John Wiley & Sons, 2000).

McRae, William, *Making a Good Thing Better: A Marriage enrichment program for small groups and couples* (Burlington, ON: Welch Publishing Company, 1985).

Miller, R.B., S. Anderson, and D. Keala, "Is Bowen Theory Valid? A review of basic research," *Journal of Marital and Family Therapy*, October 2004, Vol. 30, No. 4.

Minirith, F. and M., B. and D. Newman, and R. and S. Hemfelt, *Passages of Marriage* (Nashville, TN: Thomas Nelson Publishers, 1991).

Morgan, Dennis D., Dale H. Levandowski, and Martha L. Rogers, "The Apostle Paul: Problem formation and problem resolution from a systems perspective," *Journal of Psychology and Theology*, Summer 1981, 9(2), 136–143.

Moule, Handley, *Ephesians Studies* (London, UK: Hodder and Stoughton, 1902).

Neufeld, Thomas R. Yoder, *Ephesians: Believers church Bible commentary* (Scottsdale, PA: Herald Press, 2002).

Nichols, Michael P., *Family Therapy Concepts and Methods* (Hoboken, NJ: Pearson Education, 2008).

Olthuis, James H., *I Pledge You My Troth*, (San Francisco, CA: Harper & Row, 1975).

Osborne, Cecil G., *The Art of Understanding Your Mate* (Grand Rapid, MI: Zondervan Publishing House, 1970).

Otto, Herbert A., *Marriage and Family Enrichment: New perspectives and programs* (Nashville, TN: Abingdon, 1976).

Paolino, Thomas J. Jr., and Barbara S. McCrady (Eds.), *Marriage and Family Therapy: Psychoanalytic, behavioral and systems theory perspectives* (New York, NY: Brunner/Mazel Publishers, 1978).

Papero, Daniel V., *Bowen Family Systems Theory* (Massachusetts: Pearson 1990)

Peleg, Ora, and Meital Yitzhak, "Differentiation of Self and Separation Anxiety: Is there a similarity between spouses?" *Contemporary Family Therapy*, 2011, 33:25–36.

Peterson, Eugene, *The Message* (Colorado Springs, CO: NavPress, 2002).

Plummer, Marjorie, *From Priest's Whore to Pastor's Wife* (Burlington, VT: Ashgate Publishing Company, 2012)

Richardson, Ron, *Becoming a Healthier Pastor: Family systems theory and the pastor's own family*, (Minneapolis, MN: Augsburg Fortress, 2005).

Richardson, Ron, *Becoming Your Best: A self-help guide for thinking people* (Minneapolis, MN: Augsburg Books, 2008).

Richardson, Ron, *Couples in Conflict: A family systems approach to marriage counseling* (Minneapolis, MN: Fortress Press, 2010).

Richardson, Ron, *Creating a Healthier Church: Family systems theory, leadership, and congregational life* (Minneapolis, MN: Augsburg Fortress, 1996).

Richardson, Ron, *Family Ties that Bind* (North Vancouver, BC: Self-Counsel Press, 1984, 1995).

Richardson, Ron, *Polarization and the Healthier Church: Applying Bowen Family Theory to conflict and change in society and congregational life* (Create Space, Amazon, 2012).

Richardson, Ronald W., "Differentiation of Self as a Therapeutic Goal for the Systemic Pastoral Counselor," *Journal of Pastoral Psychotherapy*, Vol. 1(1), Fall 1987.

Roberts, Randy, "Two Distinct Approaches to Family Therapy: The ideas of Murray Bowen and Jay Haley," *The Family*, Vol. 6 No. 2, p. 42.

Rodriguez, Victor, *Bowen's Family Systems Theory Applied to Intimacy Needs in a Marriage Enrichment Program for Clergy*, DMin thesis (Denver Seminary, 2000).

Russell, Daniel Charles, *A Family Systems Understanding of Transition: Leadership succession in a faith-based organization*, DMin project (Carey Theological College, May 2009).

Steinke, Peter, Circle *of Care*, audio recording, Vol. XX, no. 2 (The College of Chaplains, Feb. 1993).

Steinke, Peter, *Congregational Leadership in Anxious Times: Being calm and courageous no matter what* (Herndon, VA: Alban Institute, 2006).

Steinke, Peter, *A Door Set Open: Grounding change in mission and hope* (Verndon, VA: Alban Institute, 2010).

Steinke, Peter, *Healthy Congregations: A Systems Approach* (Verndon, VA: Alban Institute, 1996, 2006).

Steinke, Peter, *How Your Church Family Works: Understanding congregations as emotional systems* (Herndon, VA: Alban Institute, 2006).

Steinke, Peter, *Preaching the Theology of the Cross* (Minneapolis, MN: Augsburg Publishing House, 1983).

Stevens, R. Paul, *Married for Good: The lost art of staying happily married* (Vancouver, BC: Intervarsity Press, Regent College Publishing, 1986).

Stevens, R. Paul, and Phil Collins, *The Equipping pastor* (Bethesda, MD: Alban Institute, 1993).)

Stielglitz, Gil, *Marital Intelligence* (Winona Lake, IN: BMH Books, 2010).

Stott, John, *The Message of Ephesians* (Leicester, UK: Intervarsity Press, 1979).

Ten Boom, Corrie, *The Hiding Place* (Grand Rapids, MI: Chosen Books, 1984).

Tennyson, Lord Alfred, https://www.goodreads.com/quotes/28571-if-i-had-a-flower-for-every-time-i-thought (Accessed October 17th 2017).

Thielman, Frank, *Ephesians* (Grand Rapids, MI: Baker Academic, 2010).

Thomas, Gary, *Sacred Marriage* (Grand Rapids, MI: Zondervan, 2000, 2011).

Titelman, Peter, *Clinical Applications of Bowen Family Systems Theory* (New York, NY: The Haworth Press, 1998).

Titelman, Peter (Ed.), *Emotional Cutoff: Bowen Family Systems Theory perspective* (New York, NY: The Haworth Clinical Practice Press, 2003).

Titelman, Peter, *The Therapist's Own Family: Toward the differentiation of self* (Northvale, NJ: Jason Aaronson Inc., 1987).

Titelman, Peter, *Triangles: Bowen Family Systems Theory Perspectives* (New York, NY: Haworth Press, 2008).

Tournier, Paul, *To Understand Each Other* (Richmond, VA: John Knox Press, 1962, 1972).

Trevethan, Thomas L., *Our Joyful Confidence: The lordship of Jesus in Colossians* (Downers Grove, IL: Intervarsity Press, 1981).

Turner, David L., *Matthew: Cornerstone commentary* (Carol Stream, IL: Tyndale Publishing, 2005).

Unsworth, Barry, *Crete* (Washington, DC: National Geographic Society, 2004).

Van Yperen, Jim, *Making Peace: A guide to overcoming church conflict* (Chicago IL: Moody Publishers2002).

Vogel, Ezra F., and Norman W. Bell, "The Emotionally Disturbed Child as the Family Scapegoat," in Norman W. Bell and Ezra F. Vogel (Eds.), *A Modern Introduction to the Family* (New York, NY: The Free Press, Macmillan Company, 1968).

Wallerstein, Judith, and Sandra Blakeslee, *The Good Marriage: How and why love lasts* (Boston, MA: Houghton Mifflin, 1995).

Walsh, Brian, and Sylvia C. Keesmaat, *Colossians Remixed* (Downers Grove, IL: IVP, 2004).

Wilcox, W. Bradford, and Nicholas H. Wolfinger, "Better Together: Religious attendance, gender, and relationship quality" (Institute for Family Studies, Feb. 11, 2016), https://ifstudies.org/blog/better-together-religious-attendance-gender-and-relationshIP–quality (Accessed October 17, 2017).

Williamson, Peter, *Ephesians* (Grand Rapids, MI: Baker Academics, 2009).

Wilson, Jonathan R., *God's Good World: Reclaiming the doctrine of creation* (Grand Rapids, MI: Baker Academic, 2013).

Wilson, Marvin R., *Our Father Abraham: Jewish roots of the Christian faith* (Grand Rapids, MI: Eerdmans Publishing, 1989).

Winseman, A., D. Clifton, and C. Liesvfeld, *Living Your Strengths* (New York, NY: Gallup Press, 2008).

Witte, John Jr., & Eliza Ellison (Eds.), *Covenant Marriage in Comparative Perspective* (Grand Rapids, MI: Eerdmans, 2005).

Wright, N.T., *Colossians and Philemon* (Leicester, UK: Intervarsity Press, 1986).

Endnotes

1   Names have been changed. It was not a coincidence that our St. Simon's North Van-
    couver congregation had just the day before taken a bold and costly stance for marriage.
    We believe that this wedding was a token of the Lord's favour on our new adventure in
    which we as a congregation joined the Anglican Mission in Canada, which is covered
    by thirteen African Archbishops and bishops. To learn more about this journey, you are
    invited to read Ed's earlier book Battle for the Soul of Canada.

2   Gary Thomas, *Sacred Marriage* (Zondervan Publisher, 2000, 2011, Grand Rapids, Mich-
    igan), p. 108

3   John 5:6 King James Version. Jesus asked: "Wilt Thou be made whole?"; Mark 2:17; Luke
    4:23.

4   Song of Songs 4:9.

5   Bonnie Chatwin, http://bc-counsellors.org/counsellors/bonnie-chatwin/.

6   The first part of the word *forgive* (for-) means "completely," without reservation. To
    forgive is to completely give.

7   Genesis 50:20.

8   Ray Anderson and Dennis Guernsey. *On Being Family: A Social Theology of the Family*
    (Grand Rapids MI: Eerdmans, 1985), p. 85.

9   Murray Bowen, "Theory in the Practice of Psychotherapy," in p. J. Guerin (Ed.), *Family
    Therapy: Theory and Practice* (New York, NY: Gardner Press, 1976), p. 75.

10 Anglican Mission in Canada, http://www.theamcanada.ca.

11 On Oct. 20, 2009, a Tuesday evening, Lee Grady, then editor of *Charisma Magazine*,
    came to West Point Christian Assembly, giving Ed a prophecy: "Lord, there is a well that
    you want to release in this brother and this congregation. I see a well opening up. I see a
    well of healing...."

12 1 Timothy 4:3.

13 J.O. and J.K. Balswick, *A Model for Marriage: Covenant, Grace, Empowerment, and
    Intimacy* (Downers Grove, IL: IVP Academic, 2006), p. 46; National Center for Health
    Statistics, 2005.

14 John and Anne Coles, *Making More of Marriage* (Berkhamsted, UK: New Wine Inter-
    national Publishing, 2000), pp. 61.

15 Murray Bowen, *Family Therapy in Clinical Practice* (New York, NY: Jason Aaronson
    Inc., 1985, 1983, 1978, 1992), p. 382; R. B. Miller, S. Anderson, and D. Keala, "Is Bowen
    Theory Valid? A Review of Basic Research," *Journal of Marital and Family Therapy*, Octo-
    ber 2004, Vol. 30, No. 4, 453–466.

16 Bowen's eight Family Systems Theory concepts are triangles, differentiation of self, nu-
    clear family emotional system, family projection process, multigenerational transmission
    process, emotional cutoff, sibling position, and societal emotional process. Each of the
    Family Systems concepts is defined in the glossary at the end of this book.

17 Roberta Gilbert, *Extraordinary Relationships: A new way of thinking about human inter-
    actions* (Minneapolis, MN: Chronimed Publishing, 1992), p. 61.

18 Edwin Friedman, A *Failure of Nerve Leadership in an age of the quick-fix* (Bethesda, MD:
    The Edwin Friedman Estate/Trust, 1999), p. 2.

19 Gilbert, *Extraordinary Relationships*, p. 11.

20 Ron Richardson, *Couples in Conflict: A family systems approach to marriage counseling*
    (Minneapolis, MN: Fortress Press, 2010), p. 17.

21 Paddy Ducklow, Principle #7: Ministry Is Risking Failure, https://www.vista.ubc.ca/webct/RelativeResourceManager/Template/Manual%202011%20Appendices.pdf.

22 Psalm 84:5.

23 http://www.azquotes.com/quote/786379.

24 Angus Konstam, *The History of Pirates* (New York, NY: The Lyons Press, 1999), p. 24. In the 10th century BC, the Minoan civilization was overrun by Dorian Greeks, who engaged in piratical raids using Cretan cities as bases. In Homer's Odyssey, the Cretans were described as pirates. Crete continued to be a pirate base for almost 800 years."

25 Epimenides, *Cretica*, J. Rendel Harris (Trans.), the *Expositor* (Oct. 1906, 305–17; Apr. 1907, 332–37; Apr. 1912, 348–353); Titus 1:12.

26 Barry Unsworth, *Crete*, (Washington, DC: National Geographic Society, 2004), p. 12.

27 Alpha is a great way to explore the meaning of life and faith. St. Simon's has led thirty-one Alpha Courses so far. Ed was the National Chair of Alpha Canada. https://alpha.org/

28 Gilbert, *Extraordinary Relationships*, pp. 12, 18.

29 Edwin Friedman, *Body and Soul in Family Process*, video (Pastoral Care Association of BC 4th Annual Conference, 1991).

30 Ron Richardson, *Becoming Your Best: A self-help guide for thinking people* (Minneapolis, MN: Augsburg Books, 2008), p. 100.

31 Richardson, *Couples in Conflict*, pp. 34–35.

32 Roberta Gilbert, *Extraordinary Leadership: Thinking systems, making a difference* (Virginia: Leading Systems Press, 2006), p. 26; Roberta Gilbert, *The Eight Concepts of Bowen Theory: A new way of thinking about the individual and the group* (Virginia: Leading Systems Press, 2004, 2006), p. 26.

33 Joseph C. Carolin (Ed.), *Marriage and Family Therapy: Psychoanalytic, behavioral and systems theory perspectives: Systems and spirituality: Bowen Systems Theory, faith and theology,* the papers and proceedings of a conference on theology held at Washington Theological Union (Washington, DC: July 1987), p. iii.

34 Michael E. Kerr and Murray Bowen, *Family Evaluation: An approach based on Bowen Theory* (W.W. Norton & Company, 1988), p. 192.

35 The Bowen Center for the Study of the Family, "About Murray Bowen" http://thebowencenter.org/theory/murray-bowen (Accessed Dec. 18, 2017).

36 Kerr, "Family Systems Theory and Therapy," in *Handbook of family therapy*, Gurman and Kniskern (Eds.) (New York, NY: Routledge, 1981), p. 220.

37 Friedman, *Body and Soul in Family Process*.

38 Bowen, "Theory in the Practice of Psychotherapy," p. 59; Ron Richardson, *Polarization and the Healthier Church: Applying Bowen Family Theory to conflict and change in society and congregational life* (Create Space, Amazon, 2012), p. 73.

39 Kerr and Bowen, *Family Evaluation*, p. 71: "People who have very high IQs may have their functioning totally dominated by their emotional system. A schizophrenic person, for example, can have a high IQ."

40 Bowen, *Family Therapy in Clinical Practice*, p. 354.

41 Bowen, *Family Therapy in Clinical Practice*, p. 109.

42 In John 1:12 Jesus said that as many as received him, he gave them the right to become God's children, born of God. In Revelation 3:20 Jesus is knocking at the door of our heart, inviting us to open the door so that he can come in. You can invite him by praying the following prayer: "Dear Jesus, I open the door of my heart and invite you to come in as my Lord and Saviour. I turn from selfishness and sin. Thank you for dying on the cross for my sins and rising again that I might live forever with you. Amen."

43 Edwin Friedman, *Generation to Generation* (New York, NY: The Guilford Press, 1985), p. 93; Bowen, *Family Therapy in Clinical Practice*, p. 494.

44 David S. Freeman, *Family Therapy with Couples: The family-of-origin approach* (New Jersey: Jason Aronson Inc., 1992), pp. 16, 50.

45 Ron Richardson, *Family Ties that Bind* (North Vancouver, BC: Self-Counsel Press, 1984, 1995), p. 24.

46 Bowen, "Theory in the Practice of Psychotherapy," p. 73.

47 Ed and Janice Hird, Strengthening Marriage Workshop, transcript, Session #2.

48 Bowen, *Family Therapy in Clinical Practice*, p. 504.

49 Friedman, *Generation to Generation*, p. 181.

50 Bowen, *Family Therapy in Clinical Practice*, p. 409.

51 Friedman, *Body and Soul in Family Process.*

52 Shan Fetch and Dawn McComb, "Generational Healing: A client's experience of an intervention to promote forgiveness and healing the generational bond," *Marriage and Family: A Christian Journal*, Vol. 4, Issue 2, 2001, p. 174.

53 Reggie McNeal, *A Work of Heart: Understanding how God shapes spiritual leaders* (New York, NY: John Wiley & Sons, 2011) p. 119.

54 Yasmin Hawkins, Jane Ussher, Emilee Gilbert, Janette Perz, Mirjana Sandoval, and Kendra Sundquist, "Changes in Sexuality and Intimacy After the Diagnosis and Treatment of Cancer: The experience of partners in a sexual relationship with a person with cancer" (*Cancer Nursing*, Vol. 32, No. 4, 2009) pp. 271–280.

55 Gil Stieglitz, *Marital Intelligence* (, Winona Lake, IN: BMH Books, 2010), http://www.ptlb.com. Gil breaks the top needs of the wife into the acronym HUSBAND, of which the top need, "H," is honour.

56 1 Peter 3:7 (ESV): "...showing honour to the woman ... so that your prayers will not be hindered."

57 Friedman, *Body and Soul in Family Process.*

58 Gilbert, *Extraordinary Leadership*, p. 114.

59 Richardson, *Polarization and the Healthier Church*, p. 133.

60 Roberta Gilbert, *The Cornerstone Concept: In leadership, in life* (Virginia: Leading Systems Press, 2008), p.86.

61 Friedman, *Body and Soul in Family Process*; Friedman, *Generation to Generation*, p. 69.

62 Kerr, "Family Systems Theory and Therapy," p. 263.

63 Bowen, *Family Therapy in Clinical Practice*, pp. 437, 507.

64 1 Peter 3:7 (ESV): "Likewise, husbands, live with your wives in an understanding way, showing honour to your wife..."

65 Titelman, *Emotional Cutoff: Bowen Family Systems Theory perspective* (New York, NY: The Haworth Clinical Practice Press, 2003), p. 53.

66 Richardson, *Polarization and the Healthier Church*, p. 66.

67 Quoted in Ronald W. Richardson, "Differentiation of Self as a Therapeutic Goal for the Systemic Pastoral Counselor," *Journal of Pastoral Psychotherapy*, Vol. 1(1), Fall 1987, p. 41.

68 Richardson, *Polarization and the Healthier Church*, p. 106.

69 Richardson, *Family Ties that Bind*, p. 37.

70 You can purchase *Restoring Health* on Amazon in either paperback or ebook: http://amzn.to/2D7ltDP.

71 Kerr and Bowen, *Family Evaluation*, p. 132.

72 Bowen, *Family Therapy in Clinical Practice*, p. 495.

73 Bowen, "The Use of Family Theory in Clinical Practice", *Comprehensive Psychiatry* 7:345–374, 1966, p. 173.

74 Bowen, *Family Therapy in Clinical Practice*, p. 536.

75 Bowen, "Theory in the Practice of Psychotherapy," p. 66, p. 67.

76 Gilbert, *Extraordinary Relationships*, pp. 24, 116; Paddy Ducklow, *Coaching Church Leaders in Conflict: Resolving strategies using family systems theory*, doctoral thesis, (Deerfield, IL: Trinity International University, December 2002), p. 43: "These are the qualities of maturity and the highest definition of what it is to be human in Bowen systems thought."

77 Kerr and Bowen, *Family Evaluation*, p. 77.

78 Bowen, *Family Therapy in Clinical Practice*, p. 295.

79 Bowen, *Family Therapy in Clinical Practice*, p. 111.

80 Michael P. Nichols, *Family Therapy Concepts and Methods* (Hoboken, NJ: Pearson Education, 2008), p. 143.

81 Bowen, "Theory in the Practice of Psychotherapy," p. 56–57; Murray Bowen, *The Origins of Family Psychotherapy: The NIMH family study project* (J. Butler, ed.) (Lanham, MD: Jason Aronson, 2013, pp. 43, 163.

82 Bowen, *Family Therapy in Clinical Practice*, p. 84.

83 Psalm 139:7.

84 Kerr, "Family Systems Theory and Therapy,"p.243.

85 Ona Cohn Bregman, "Preface," in O.C. Bregman and C.M. White (Eds.) *Bringing Systems Thinking to Life: Expanding the horizons for Bowen Family Systems Theory*, (New York, NY: Routledge Taylor & Francis Group, 2011), p. xx.

86 Edwin Friedman, *Bowen Theory and Therapy*, (PsycINFO Database Record (c) 2012 APA), p. 149. https://www.researchgate.net/publication/232485321_Bowen_theory_and_therapy (Accessed January 23, 2018), p. 162.

87 Bowen, "Theory in the Practice of Psychotherapy," p. 86; Friedman, *Bowen Theory and Therapy*, p. 149.

88 Murray Bowen, "Various Theoretical Points People Miss: A training session by Dr. Murray Bowen at the Minnesota Institute of Family Dynamics," in O.C. Bregman and C. M. White (Eds.), *Bringing Systems Thinking to Life* (New York, NY: Routledge Taylor & Francis Group, 2011), p. 43: "When you try to change your fellow human being, you are a malignancy."

89 Bowen, "Theory in the Practice of Psychotherapy," p. 448.

90 Herbert A. Otto, *Marriage and Family Enrichment: New perspectives and programs* (Nashville, TN: Abingdon, 1976).

91 Michael Fulwiler, "Managing Conflict: Solvable versus perpetual problems," The Gottman Relationship Blog, https://www.gottman.com/blog/managing-conflict-solvable-vs-perpetual-problems/; Ellie Lisitsa, "The Four Horsemen," https://www.gottman.com/blog/category/column/the-four-horsemen (Accessed Oct. 20, 2017).

92 Nugent, Tom, "The Einstein of Love," *FDU Magazine*, Winter/Spring 2017 Edition, https://medium.com/@FDUMagazine/the-einstein-of-love-ad28bc86dode (Accessed Dec. 25, 2017).

93 Bowen, *The Origins of Family Psychotherapy*, pp. 36, 51.

94 Kerr and Bowen, *Family Evaluation*, p. 187.

95 Bowen, "Theory in the Practice of Psychotherapy," p. 86.

96 Bowen, *Family Therapy in Clinical Practice*, p. 443.

97 Richardson, *Couples in Conflict*, p. 22 "Pursuing and distancing, in overt or subtle ways, is a dance performed in nearly every close relationship in an attempt to deal with the two life forces of togetherness and individuality."

98 Hird, Strengthening Marriage Workshop, transcript, Session #4.

99 Kerr and Bowen, *Family Evaluation*, p. 186.
100 Friedman, *Failure of Nerve*, p. 305.
101 Hird, Strengthening Marriage Workshop, Session 4.
102 Nichols, *Family Therapy Concepts and Methods*, p. 126.
103 Kerr and Bowen, *Family Evaluation*, p. 7.
104 Peter Steinke, *How Your Church Family Works: Understanding congregations as emotional systems* (Herndon, VA: Alban Institute, 2006), p. 10.
105 Steinke, Peter, *Congregational Leadership in Anxious Times: Being calm and courageous no matter what* (Herndon, VA: Alban Institute, 2006), p. 25.
106 www.edhird.com.
107 Bowen, *Origins of Family Psychotherapy*, pp. 51, 160.
108 Amos 3:3 (KJV): "Can two walk together, except they be agreed?"
109 Kerr and Bowen, *Family Evaluation*, p.47: "Undifferentiated people typically blame or cut off rather than face the problem and working through."
110 Ron Richardson, *Becoming a Healthier Pastor: Family systems theory and the pastor's own family* (Minneapolis, MN: Augsburg Fortress, 2005), p. 19.
111 Nichols, *Family Therapy Concepts and Methods*, p. 146.
112 Ron Richardson, *Creating a Healthier Church: Family systems theory, leadership, and congregational life* (Minneapolis, MN: Augsburg Fortress, 1996), p. 91.
113 Richardson, *Family Ties that Bind*, p. 33
114 Isaiah 29:13; Matthew 15:8.
115 Bowen, "Theory in the Practice of Psychotherapy," p. 68.
116 Richardson, *Family Ties that Bind*, p. 33.
117 Balswick, *A Model for Marriage*, p. 64.
118 Bowen, "Theory in the Practice of Psychotherapy," pp. 68, 73.
119 2 Chronicles 36:13.
120 Mark 3:5.
121 Mark 6:52, 8:17; Ephesians 4:18: "They are darkened in their understanding ... due to the hardening of their hearts."
122 Cecil G. Osborne, *The Art of Understanding Your Mate* (Grand Rapids, MI: Zondervan Publishing House, 1970), p. 12.
123 Lord Alfred Tennyson, https://www.goodreads.com/quotes/28571-if-i-had-a-flower-for-every-time-i-thought (Accessed October 17, 2017).
124 Robert Browning, "Rabbi Ben Ezra," https://www.poetryfoundation.org/poems/43775/rabbi-ben-ezra (Accessed October 17, 2017).
125 Bowen defined his last Family Systems Theory concept 'emotional cutoff' as the process of separation, isolation, withdrawal, running away, or denying the importance of the parental family.
126 Gilbert, *Extraordinary Relationships*, p. 64.
127 Stephanie J. Ferrera, "The Continuum of Emotional Cutoff in Divorce," in Peter Titelman (Ed.), *Emotional Cutoff: Bowen Family Systems Theory perspective* (New York, NY: The Haworth Clinical Practice Press, 2003), p. 311.
128 Peter Titelman (Ed.), *Emotional Cutoff: Bowen Family Systems Theory perspective* (New York, NY: The Haworth Clinical Practice Press, 2003), *Emotional Cutoff*, p. 56.
129 Richardson, *Becoming a Healthier Pastor*, p. 87: "They may see it in a triangular way as a betrayal of their own position and say, 'You are going over to the enemy.'"
130 Corrie Ten Boom, *The Hiding Place* (Grand Rapids, MI: Chosen Books, 1984).
131 Phil Klever, "Marital Functioning and Multigenerational Fusion and Cutoff," in Titelman, *Emotional Cutoff*, pp. 238, 239.

132 Steinke, *How Your Church Family Works,* p. 28.

133 Priscilla J. Friesen, "Emotional Cutoff and the Brain," in Titelman, *Emotional Cutoff,* p. 91.

134 Titelman, *Emotional Cutoff,* pp. 135, 146, 155.

135 Bowen, "Various Theoretical Points People Miss," p. 46.

136 Titelman, *Emotional Cutoff,* p. 22.

137 Richardson, *Couples in Conflict,* p. 196.

138 Bowen, *Family Therapy in Clinical Practice,* p. 433.

139 Nichols, *Family Therapy Concepts and Methods,* p. 146.

140 Bowen, *Family Therapy in Clinical Practice,* p.540: "The effort to help or to supervise someone in this effort has been called 'coaching' because it is so similar to the relationship of a coach to an athlete who is working to improve his athletic ability."

141 Bowen, *The Origins of Family Psychotherapy,* p. 69.

142 Friedman, *Generation to Generation,* p. 293.

143 Kerr and Bowen, *Family Evaluation,* p. 319.

144 Kerr and Bowen, *Family Evaluation,* p. 192; Bowen, *Family Therapy in Clinical Practice,* p. 476.

145 Kerr and Bowen, *Family Evaluation,* p. 87.

146 Gilbert, *Extraordinary Leadership,* p.84, p. 104.

147 Kerr and Bowen, *Family Evaluation,* p. 182.

148 Matthew 7:3–5 (NIV): "Why do you see the speck that is in your brother's eye, but do not notice the log that is in your own eye? Or how can you say to your brother, 'Let me take the speck out of your eye,' when there is the log in your own eye? You hypocrite, first take the log out of your own eye, and then you will see clearly to take the speck out of your brother's eye."

149 Bowen, *Family Therapy in Clinical Practice,* pp. 402, 480.

150 Daniel Papero, *Bowen Family Systems Theory* (Massachusetts: Pearson 1990), p. 74.

151 Kerr and Bowen, *Family Evaluation,* p. 18; Gilbert, *The Cornerstone Concept,* p. 71; Gilbert, *Extraordinary Relationships,* p. 121; Bowen, *The Origins of Family Psychotherapy,* p. 159.

152 2 Corinthians 4:1, 16: "Therefore, … we do not lose heart."

153 Richardson, *Family Ties that Bind,* p. 38.

154 Kerr and Bowen, p. 150.

155 "Various Theoretical Points People Miss: A Training Session by Dr. Murray Bowen at the Minnesota Institute of Family Dynamics", G. Mary Bourne, Ed., *Bringing Systems Thinking to Life,* Bregman and White, p. 47.

156 Kerr and Bowen, *Family Evaluation,* p. 203 "Objectivity about one's parents (the ultimate resolution of the transference or unresolved emotional attachment to one's family) promotes objectivity about oneself. A reasonable amount of objectivity about self and others, coupled with the ability to act on that basis of objectivity when it is important to do so, is the essence of differentiation of self."

157 Hird, Strengthening Marriage Workshop, transcript.

158 Peter Titelman, *Clinical Applications of Bowen Family Systems Theory* (New York, NY: The Haworth Press, 1998), p. 44.

159 Roberta M. Gilbert, *The Eight Concepts,* p. 99.

160 Nichols, *Family Therapy Concepts and Methods,* p. 147.

161 Kerr and Bowen, *Family Evaluation,* p. 188.

162 Richardson, *Couples in Conflict,* pp. 22, 72.

163 Richardson, "Differentiation of Self," p. 36.

164 Paddy Ducklow, Conflicted Church/Conflicted Leader course, Carey Theological College, Fall 2011.

165 Psalm 139:23.

166 1 Samuel 16:7.

167 Psalm 26:2. Self-examination is one of the six Lenten disciplines: Prayer, fasting, self-examination, repentance, bible-reading, generosity, especially to the poor. These six disciplines are not meant only for Lent but rather especially for Lent.

168 Eddie Espinosa, "Change My Heart, O God,"(Vineyard Music, 1995) https://www. youtube.com/watch?v=DwudqCO7mSQ (Accessed October 24, 2017).

169 Titelman, *Clinical Applications of Bowen Family Systems Theory*, p. 8.

170 Nichols, *Family Therapy Concepts and Methods*, p. 140.

171 Richardson, *Couples in Conflict*, p. 12.

172 Friedman, *Body and Soul in Family Process*.

173 Friedman, *Body and Soul in Family Process*.

174 Friedman, *Bowen Theory and Therapy*, p. 155 "But the major 'technique' that Bowen and his disciples have taught as the way to maintain such objectivity – and a differentiation-promoting position- is simply to ask questions."

175 Bowen, *Family Therapy in Clinical Practice*, p. 314.

176 Richardson, *Polarization and the Healthier Church*, p. 121.

177 Steinke, *How Your Church Family Works*, p. 98.

178 Kerr and Bowen, *Family Evaluation*, p. 154: "When anxiety is that high, the goal is to stay in contact with people, but not let the anxiety dictate one's actions"; Gilbert, *The Cornerstone Concept*, p. 61: "At the same time he or she does not distance, but stays in good communication with everyone."

179 Luke 15: 11-32.

180 Friedman, *Bowen Theory and Therapy*, p. 157.

181 Papero, "Bowen Family Systems and Marriage," p. 17.

182 Murray Bowen, "The Use of Family Theory in Clinical Practice," p. 168.

183 Kerr and Bowen, *Family Evaluation*, pp. 56, 57.

184 Friedman, *Body and Soul in Family Process*: "I know how to destroy another person, by overfunctioning in their space."

185 Bowen, "The Use of Family Theory in Clinical Practice," pp. 168, 352.

186 Richardson, *Becoming Your Best*, pp. 101, 102.

187 Richardson, *Becoming a Healthier Pastor* p.32.

188 Richardson, *Polarization and the Healthier Church*, p. 54.

189 Bowen, *Family Therapy in Clinical Practice*, p. 85.

190 Gilbert, *Extraordinary Relationships*, p. 45.

191 Friedman VHS video, the Pastoral Care Association of BC 4th Annual Conference, 1991 "Body and Soul in Family Process".

192 Bowen, *Family Therapy in Clinical Practice*, p. 362.

193 Selden Dunbar Illick, et al., "Toward Understanding and Measuring Emotional Cutoff," in Titelman, *Emotional Cutoff*, p. 205: "Bowen's (1978) reference to having 'the ability to see one's own family more as people than emotionally endowed images' (p. 531) is important."

194 Kerr and Bowen, *Family Evaluation*, p. 28.

195 Gilbert, *The Cornerstone Concept*, p. 92.

196 Randy Roberts, "Two Distinct Approaches to Family Therapy: The Ideas of Murray Bowen and Jay Haley," *The Family*, Vol. 6 No. 2, p. 42.

197 Gilbert, *The Cornerstone Concept*, p. 87.

198 Gilbert, *Extraordinary Relationships*, pp. 5, 15.

199 Gilbert, *Extraordinary Relationships*, p. 113.

200 Murray, "Various Theoretical Points People Miss," p. 44: "The more immature the person, the more that person acts like God. That's like they know something they don't."

201 Balswick, *A Model for Marriage*, p. 24.

202 Diana R. Garland, *Family Ministry: A Comprehensive Guide,* (Downers Grove, IL: IVP Academic, 1999), p. 539, quoting David Elkind: "Partners now seek in their mates the qualities once sought in God."

203 Gilbert, *Extraordinary Relationships*, p. 19.

204 Richardson, *Family Ties that Bind*, p. 40.

205 Bowen, *Family Therapy in Clinical Practice*, p. 291.

206 Titelman, *Emotional Cutoff,* p. 21.

207 Friedman, *Failure of Nerve*, p. 23.

208 Bowen, *Family Therapy in Clinical Practice*, p. 434.

209 Bowen, "Theory in the Practice of Psychotherapy," p. 49.

210 Friedman, *Failure of Nerve*, p. 8.

211 Bowen, *The Origins of Family Psychotherapy,* pp. 39, 69, 100, 113, 118.

212 Bowen, *Family Therapy in Clinical Practice*, p. 113.

213 Bowen, *The Origins of Family Psychotherapy,* p. 70.

214 Richardson, *Becoming Your Best*, p.2.

215 Exodus 20:12; Matthew 15:5-7; Ephesians 6:2.

216 Hird, Strengthening Marriage Workshop, transcript, Session #2.

217 Bowen, *Family Therapy in Clinical Practice*, p. 518.

218 Matthew 19:8.

219 Richardson, *Couples in Conflict*, pp. 138, 139, 140, 186.

220 Bowen, *Family Therapy in Clinical Practice*, p. 543.

221 Friedman, *Generation to Generation*, pp. 178, 302.

222 Gilbert, *Extraordinary Relationships*, p. 121.

223 Bowen, *Family Therapy in Clinical Practice*, p. 518.

224 Bowen, *Family Therapy in Clinical Practice*, p. 502.

225 Eileen Gotlieb, "Emotional Cutoff and Holocaust Survivors," in Titelman, *Emotional Cutoff,* p. 430.

226 Richardson, *Becoming a Healthier Pastor,* p. 87.

227 Kerr and Bowen, *Family Evaluation*, p. 287.

228 Bowen, *Family Therapy in Clinical Practice*, p. 494: "I have never seen a family in which the 'emotional fusion' is not present."

229 Malachi 4:6; Luke 1:17.

230 Friedman, *Bowen Theory and Therapy*, p. 148.

231 Bowen, *Family Therapy in Clinical Practice,* pp. 516, 517.

232 Kerr and Bowen, *Family Evaluation*, p. 157.

233 Nichols, *Family Therapy Concepts and Methods*, p. 144.

234 Friedman, *Failure of Nerve*, p. 12.

235 Richardson, *Family that Bind Ties*, p. 104: "It is not unusual for cutoffs from the family to occur at the time of death as a way of trying to escape the new triangles."

236 Bowen, *Family Therapy in Clinical Practice*, p. 542

237 Gilbert, *The Cornerstone Concept*, p. 63.

238 Bowen, *Family Therapy in Clinical Practice*, p. 542.

239 Friedman, *Bowen Theory and Therapy*, p. 163.

240 Richardson, *Becoming a Healthier Pastor*, p. 43

241 Richardson, Ron, *Family Ties that Bind* (Self-Counsel Press, North Vancouver, BC, 1984, 1995). During our Strengthening Marriage workshop, we gave this book to each couple as a graduation gift.

242 Nichols, *Family Therapy Concepts and Methods*, p.147.

243 Bowen, "Theory in the Practice of Psychotherapy," pp. 52, 76; Bowen, *Family Systems Theory*, p. 40.

244 Bowen, *Family Therapy in Clinical Practice*, p. 501.

245 Titelman, *Emotional Cutoff*, p. 23. "Cutoff is not created or sustained by a single individual. It takes two or more individuals to sustain a cutoff. In addition, it takes at least one parent and a child for a process of cutoff to occur."

246 Gilbert, *Extraordinary Relationships*, p. 30 "The more one can see the systems-of-triangles perspective, the less prone one will be to take sides, to take things personally, to take thoughtless positions, or to assign blame."

247 Kerr and Bowen, *Family Evaluation*, pp. 138, 146.

248 Bowen, *Family Therapy in Clinical Practice*, p. 499: "Most people cannot tolerate more than a few minutes on a personal level."

249 Susan L. Jones, *Family Therapy: A comparison of approaches* (Bowie, MD: Robert Brady Co., 1980), p. 48; Bowen, *Family Therapy in Clinical Practice*, p. 401.

250 Bowen, *Family Therapy in Clinical Practice*, p. 349: "A disturbed family is always looking for a vulnerable outsider."

251 Bowen, *Family Therapy in Clinical Practice*, 1974, p. 530.

252 Kerr and Bowen, *Family Evaluation*, p. 139.

253 Kerr and Bowen, *Family Evaluation*, p. 135.

254 Nichols, *Family Therapy Concepts and Methods*, p. 146.

255 Kerr and Bowen, *Family Evaluation*, p. 139.

256 Titelman, *Clinical Applications of Family Systems Theory* (New York, NY: The Haworth Press, 1998), p. 10.

257 Friedman, *Bowen Theory and Therapy*, 1991, p. 150.

258 Exodus 25:30; 39:30; Numbers 4:7; 1 Samuel 21:6; 1 Kings 7:48; 2 Chronicles 4:19.

259 2 Kings 23:3; 2 Chronicles 34:31.

260 Acts 2:28.

261 Nichols, *Family Therapy Concepts and Methods*, p. 136.

262 Michael E. Kerr, "Chronic Anxiety and Defining a Self," *The Atlantic Monthly*, Sept. 1988, p. 58.

263 Bowen, *Family Therapy in Clinical Practice*, p. 349.

264 Richardson, *Couples in Conflict*, p. 65.

265 Kerr and Bowen, *Family Evaluation*, p. 153, Ft 10.

266 Kerr and Bowen, *Family Evaluation*, p. 161.

267 Bowen, *Family Therapy in Clinical Practice*, p. 349.

268 Bowen, *Family Evaluation*, pp. 12, 509.

269 Bowen, *Family Therapy in Clinical Practice*, p. 520,

270 R. Paul Stevens, *Married for Good: The lost art of staying happily married* (Vancouver, BC: Intervarsity Press, Regent College Publishing, 1986), p. 17.

271 Bowen, *Family Therapy in Clinical Practice*, p. 279.

272 Ed Hird, "Rationale for the Wedding Service" (Vancouver, BC: Vancouver School of Theology, 1977), p. 3 (drawn and adapted from a service in *The Abingdon Marriage Manual*, p. 130 and from *Christian Perspectives on Sex and Marriage*): "The 2nd theme in the marriage service of submission/self-giving is explored in a way that uses the Philippians 2:5–11 hymn as a pattern for the often-overlooked submission that both partners

are called to;" Janice and Ed Hird's Order of Wedding Service, May 21, 1977, Brighouse United Church, Richmond.

273 Meredith G. Kline, *The Structure of Biblical Authority* (Grand Rapids, MI: Baker Books, 1975), p.25.

274 Marvin R. Wilson, *Our Father Abraham: Jewish roots of the Christian faith* (Grand Rapids, MI: Eerdmans Publishing, 1989), p. 203: "The covenant ceremony of marriage was seen as a replica or reenactment of what happened at Sinai"; John Stott, *The Message of Ephesians*, (Leicester, UK: Intervarsity Press, 1979), p. 226: "Already in the Old Testament the gracious covenant which God made with his people Israel was many times referred to as a marriage covenant. E.g. Is. 54:5-8; Jer. 2:1–3; 31:31–32; Ezek. 23; Hos. 1–3."

275 Michael S. Horton, *Covenant and Eschatology: The divine drama* (Louisville, KY: Westminster John Knox Press, 2002), p. 93.

276 Balswick, *A Model for Marriage*, p. 30-31. Like with our marriages, the Trinity is a dynamic dance of particularity and relatedness without absorption.

277 Ephesians 1:6.

278 Stieglitz, *Marital Intelligence*.

279 Galatians 5:1.

280 Stevens, *Married for Good*, p. 47.

281 Eugene Peterson, *The Message* (Colorado Springs, CO: NavPress, 2002).

282 *The Book of Common Prayer* (Toronto: Anglican Book Centre, 1962), p. 564; see also p. 567: "…signifying unto us the mystical union which is between Christ and his Church. This holy estate Christ adorned and beautified with his presence, and first miracle that he wrought, in Cana of Galilee."

283 Stevens, *Married for Good*, p. 24.

284 Steinke, *Congregational Leadership in Anxious Times*, p. 27.

285 Song of Songs 8:6.

286 Stevens, *Married for Good*, p. 20.

287 Anderson and Guernsey, *On Being Family*, pp. 50, 89.

288 2 Chronicles 15:12. "They entered into a covenant to seek the Lord, the God of their ancestors, with all their heart and soul."

289 Leviticus 19: 18; Mark 12:30–31.

290 Michael S. Horton, *Lord and Servant: A covenant Christology* (Louisville, KY: Westminster John Knox Press, 2005), pp. 4, 21: "A theology of pilgrims will have to suffice—and does suffice, for meeting a Stranger."

291 Peter Williamson, *Ephesians* (Grand Rapids, MI: Baker Academics, 2009), p. 174.

292 Thomas R. Yoder Neufeld, *Ephesians: Believers church Bible commentary*, pp. 243, 255; Frank Thielman, *Ephesians* (Grand Rapids, MI: Baker Academic, 2010), p. 365.

293 2nd Corinthians 3:17.

294 E. Stanley Jones, *Victory Through Surrender* (Nashville, TN: Abingdon Publications, 1980), p. 127–128.

295 Bowen, *Family Theory in Practice*, p. 360.

296 Stott, *The Message of Ephesians*, p. 215

297 Williamson, *Ephesians*, p.158.

298 Neufeld, *Ephesians*, p. 257.

299 F.F. Bruce, *The Epistle to the Ephesians*, (London, UK: Pickering & Inglis Ltd, 1961), p. 113.

300 Stott, *Message of Ephesians*, p. 215.

301 Stott, *Message of Ephesians*, p. 219.

302 Stott, *Message of Ephesians*, p. 221.

303 Thielman, *Ephesians,* p. 376: "[*Kephale* 's] precise meaning is not self-evident. It was not commonly used in ancient Greek as a metaphor for an authority or leader."

304 Friedman, *Bowen Theory and Therapy,* p. 154, quoting Bowen.

305 2 Chronicles 32:36; Obadiah 1:3.

306 Stott, *Message of Ephesians,* p. 227; also, p. 226: "Jesus … boldly referred to himself as the Bridegroom (Mark 2:18—20; John 3:29). Paul enlarges on that image … in 2 Corinthians 11:1–3."

307 The closest Hebrew word to *agape* is *ahava,* used in Leviticus 19:18 to love your neighbour as yourself and in Deuteronomy 6:5 to love God. *Hesed* is a related word speaking of God's covenant faithfulness. Both are needed in a healthy marriage.

308 Harold W. Hoehner, *Ephesians Cornerstone Biblical Commentary* (Carol Stream, IL: Tyndale, 2008), p.115; see also Markus Barth, *Ephesians 4–6: The anchor Bible* (Garden City, NY: Double Day & Company Inc., 1974).

309 Williamson, *Ephesians,* p. 162, quoting A. Murray (transl.), *Private Orations III,* Loeb Classical Library (Boston: Harvard, 1939), p. 445–46.

310 Thielman, *Ephesians,* pp. 371, 392.

311 Stieglitz, *Marital Intelligence.* Gil speaks of RADICAL women who show respect to their husbands by digging for their strengths.

312 Kyle Benson, "The Magic Art of Relationships According to Science", October 4, 2017. https://www.gottman.com/blog/the-magic-relationshIP–ratio-according-science/ (Accessed Oct. 17, 2017).

313 Bruce, *Epistle to the Ephesians,* p. 117.

314 1 Peter 3:4 (NIV).

315 Revelation 21:2 (NIV): "I saw the Holy City, the new Jerusalem, coming down out of heaven from God, prepared as a bride beautifully dressed for her husband"; (KJV): "… prepared as a bride adorned for her husband."

316 Williamson, *Ephesians,* p. 173.

317 Stott, *Meaning of Ephesians,* p. 231; Thielman, *Ephesians,* p. 389.

318 W. Bradford Wilcox and Nicholas H. Wolfinger, "Better Together: Religious attendance, gender, and relationship quality" (Institute for Family Studies, Feb. 11, 2016), https://ifstudies.org/blog/better-together-religious-attendance-gender-and-relationshIP–quality (Accessed October 17, 2017).

319 Richardson, *Creating a Healthy Church,* p. 182; Richardson *Becoming a Healthier Pastor,* p. 67.

320 Gilbert, *Eight Concepts,* p. 40: "Martin Luther's famous statement, 'Here I stand!' would be an example of how the guiding principles operate to direct basic self."

321 Ducklow, *Coaching Church Leaders in Conflict,* p. 232.

322 Gilbert, *Eight Concepts,* p. 118.

323 Nichols, *Family Therapy Concepts and Methods,* p. 316.

324 Randall T. Frost, "Thinking Systems in Pastoral Training," in Bregman and White (Eds.), *Bringing Systems Thinking to Life* (New York, NY: Routledge, 2010), pp. 192–193.

325 Richardson, *Polarization and the Healthier Church,* p. 8; Richardson, *Couples in Conflict,* p. 235; Gilbert, *Cornerstone Concept,* pp. 51, 103.

326 Michael F. Haverluck, "Sweet 60: Billy Graham one of 10 "Most Admired Men' again," One News Now, January 8, 2017, https://www.onenewsnow.com/culture/2017/01/08/sweet-60-billy-graham-one-of-10-most-admired-men-again (Accessed October 29, 2017); http://lightmagazine.ca/2017/02/rising-love-a-valentines-story.

327 Biography.com, Billy Graham Biography, http://www.biography.com/people/billy-graham-9317669 (Accessed October 29, 2017).

328 Patricia Daniels Cornwell, *A Time for Remembering: The Ruth Bell Graham story* (San Francisco: Harper & Row, 1983), p. 60.

329 Cornwell, *A Time for Remembering*, p. 61.

330 Cornwell, *A Time for Remembering*, p. 63.

331 Cornwell, *A Time for Remembering*, p. 65.

332 Cornwell, *A Time for Remembering*, p. 67.

333 Cornwell, *A Time for Remembering*, p. 72.

334 Cornwell, *A Time for Remembering*, p. 155.

335 Cornwell, *A Time for Remembering*, p. 78.

336 Cornwell, *A Time for Remembering*, p. 79.

337 Cornwell, *A Time for Remembering*, p. 194.

338 Cornwell, *A Time for Remembering*, p. 149.

339 Bowen, *Family Therapy in Clinical Practice,* p. 204: "[N]either gives in to the other on major issues. These marriages are intense in terms of the amount of emotional energy each invests in the other."